Own iT! 2

A2 Key (for schools) test content in *Own It!* Level 2 has been checked by Cambridge Assessment English for accuracy and level.

STUDENT'S BOOK
WITH DIGITAL PACK

Claire Thacker and Stuart Cochrane
with Andrew Reid and Daniel Vincent

CONTENTS

STARTER

WELCOME!

 **LEARN TO LEARN**

Verb and noun phrases

We often use verbs and nouns together to make different phrases. Learn them together.

VOCABULARY

Free time and hobbies

🎧 S.01 **1** Match verbs 1–11 with the words in the box to make phrases. Listen, check and repeat.

a bike ride	a blog	an instrument
books/magazines	cakes/videos	friends
music	~~online~~	photos
shopping	songs	

1 chat _online_
2 download _____
3 go _____
4 go for _____
5 hang out with _____
6 listen to _____
7 make _____
8 play _____
9 read _____
10 take _____
11 write _____

🎧 S.02 **2** Listen and write the activities in Exercise 1.

1 _play an instrument_
2 _____
3 _____
4 _____
5 _____
6 _____
7 _____

Sport

🎧 S.03 **3** Match the words with the pictures 1–8. Circle the two sports that aren't in the pictures. Listen, check and repeat.

athletics	☐	basketball	☐
gymnastics	1	hockey	☐
rugby	☐	sailing	☐
swimming	☐	table tennis	☐
volleyball	☐	windsurfing	☐

4 Complete the list with nouns in Exercises 1 and 3.

Verb	Noun
play	_an instrument,_
go	
make	
write	
read	

Use it!

5 Discuss the questions.

1 What is your favourite sport to watch on TV?
2 What is your favourite sport to do?
3 What isn't a good sport to do on your own?

Explore it! 🖱

Is the sentence *T* (true) or *F* (false)?

Rugby is popular in many countries, but it is the only sport in Exercise 3 that isn't played at the Summer Olympic Games. ☐

Find another interesting fact about sports and write a question for your partner to answer.

READING
A blog post

1 Look at the photos in the blog post. What do you want to know about the people?

 S.04

2 Read the blog post. Do you learn the information you wanted to know in Exercise 1?

3 Find words in the blog post that mean:
1 doing a lot of things _busy_
2 difficult _____
3 making you a bit angry _____
4 very bad _____
5 very good _____

4 Read the blog post again and write the names of the people. Who …
1 is a busy person? _Rosie_
2 are Rosie's brother and sister? _____
3 likes computer magazines and computer games? _____
4 is not a good singer? _____
5 are Sara and Fatima? _____
6 thinks Rosie's blog is very good? _____

🔊 Voice it!

5 Discuss the questions.
1 Are you like any of the people in Rosie's blog? If so, who and why?
2 Do you read blogs? Why / Why not?
3 What's your favourite blog? What's it about?

THOUGHTS FOR TODAY

Rosie Wilson

Hi everyone! Today, my blog is all about my hobbies, family and friends. I'm always busy! So, what do I do?

I go swimming three mornings a week. I always get up at 5.30 am 😴. It's tough, but swimming is my favourite thing (after my blog – obviously!).

My big brother, Dan

He plays computer games and he sometimes reads magazines (computer game ones!). He plays football every day with his friends, but he doesn't leave the house! 😒

My annoying little sister, Nora

She does her homework and she often listens to music at the same time. Does she sing too? Yes, she does – but she's a terrible singer! 😱

Best friends forever: Sara and Fatima 🖤🖤🖤

I don't see them during the week because we don't go to the same school. That isn't a problem because we usually hang out together at the weekend. They love taking selfies and they post Snapchat stories every day!

What about you? Do you often read my blog? How do you spend your free time? **Let me know!**

COMMENTS:

Jody I read your blog in my free time. It's brilliant!

LANGUAGE IN ACTION
Present simple

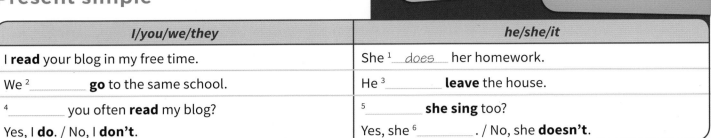

Watch video S.1
What does Zara do on the bus?
What does the vlogger do in the morning?

I/you/we/they	he/she/it
I **read** your blog in my free time.	She ¹ _does_ her homework.
We ² _____ **go** to the same school.	He ³ _____ **leave** the house.
⁴ _____ you often **read** my blog? Yes, I **do**. / No, I **don't**.	⁵ _____ **she sing** too? Yes, she ⁶ _____ . / No, she **doesn't**.

1 Complete the examples in the table above. Use the blog post on page 5 to help you.

2 Write present simple sentences.

1 Rosie / get up / at 5.30 am three mornings a week.
   Rosie gets up at 5.30 am three mornings a week.

2 Dan / not play / computer games. _____

3 Nora / not listen / to music when she / do / her homework. _____

4 Sara and Fatima / not see / Rosie during the week. _____

S.05 **3** Complete the blog post with the present simple form of the verbs. Then listen and check.

I ¹ _like_ (like) my new school. I ² _____ (not know) all the students in my class yet, but I ³ _____ (sit) next to a boy called Jorge in my English class. He's sports mad. He ⁴ _____ (play) basketball every day. On some days he ⁵ _____ (not have) lunch – he's on the basketball court!

⁶ _____ you _____ (get) a lot of homework? Our teachers ⁷ _____ (give) us lots! I ⁸ _____ (not do) it at home – I ⁹ _____ (go) to homework club on Wednesdays. Some of the older students ¹⁰ _____ (help) us. They're nice. After homework club, I ¹¹ _____ (not get) home until about 6.30 pm. I ¹² _____ (listen) to music and relax before dinner.

Adverbs of frequency

Rosie is **always** busy.
Dan **sometimes** reads magazines.
Nora **often** listens to music when she does her homework.
Rosie **usually** hangs out with friends at the weekend.

4 Complete the timeline with the adverbs of frequency in the table above.

0%	¹ _____	³ _____	100%
never	² _____	⁴ _____	

5 Write the sentences with the words in brackets.

1 I'm late for school. (never)
   I'm never late for school.

2 I do my homework at the weekend. (always) _____

3 Do you go shopping with friends? (sometimes) _____

4 I'm tired after school. (often) _____

5 Do you take photos on your phone? (usually) _____

Use it!

6 Discuss the sentences in Exercise 5. Are they true for you?

Are you always late for school?

No, I'm never late for school!

VOCABULARY AND LISTENING
Personal possessions

🎧 **1** Match the words with the photos. Listen, check
S.06   and repeat.

bus pass	☐	camera	☐
headphones	☐	keys	☐
laptop	☐	money	☐
passport	☐	phone	☐
portable charger	☐	tablet	1

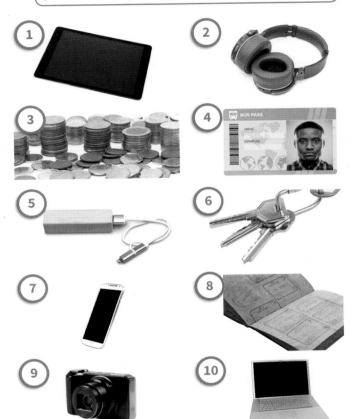

2 Complete the sentences with words in Exercise 1.

1 Where are my _keys_ ? I can't open the door.

2 Dan is always late. Can I borrow your _____
   to message him?

3 You can't go to the USA without your
   _____ .

4 I want to take good photos. I need a nice
   _____ .

5 That music is very loud. Use your _____ .

🛡 LEARN TO LEARN
Making vocabulary cards
Make vocabulary cards to help you learn new words.
Draw a picture on one side and write the word on the
other.

3 Make your own vocabulary cards for the words
   in Exercise 1.

💬 **4** Test a partner. Show your cards. Can your
   partner say the words in English?

🔵 **Use it!**

5 Describe a possession in Exercise 1 for your
   partner to guess. Think about:
   - when you use it
   - where you use it
   - what you use it for.

   > I use it every day. I always keep it
   > in my bag. I use it to get to school.

   > Is it your bus pass?

A conversation

🎧 **6** Listen. Circle the club Alex wants to go to.
S.07
   a coding club   b photography club

🎧 **7** Listen again and circle the correct answers.
S.07
   1 Emine goes to the … club.
     a coding   b (photography)
   2 Alex … taking photos.
     a likes   b doesn't like
   3 Alex has got a … .
     a tablet   b laptop
   4 Mr Adams … .
     a is a good teacher   b knows Bill Gates
   5 In her free time, Libby writes … .
     a a blog   b computer programs

🔵 **Voice it!**

8 Do you go to any school clubs? Which ones?
   What school club would you like to go to?

LANGUAGE IN ACTION

love, like, don't mind, hate + -ing

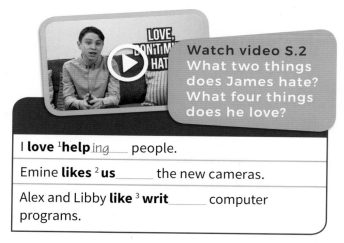

Watch video S.2
What two things does James hate? What four things does he love?

I **love** [1]**help** *ing* people.	
Emine **likes** [2]**us** _____ the new cameras.	
Alex and Libby **like** [3]**writ**_____ computer programs.	

1 Complete the words in the table above.

2 Write the sentences with the correct form of the verbs.

1 Emine likes _meeting_ (meet) new people.
2 Alex doesn't like _____ (take) photos.
3 Libby doesn't mind _____ (help) Alex.
4 Mr Adams loves _____ (tell) stories.

3 Complete the blog post with the correct form of the verbs in the boxes.

> love ☺☺☺   like ☺   not mind ☺
> not like ☹   hate ☹☹☹

> do   get up   help   ~~listen~~   speak

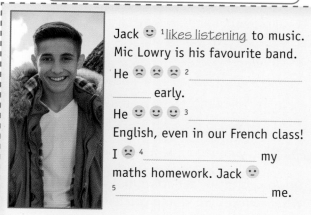

Jack ☺ [1]_likes listening_ to music. Mic Lowry is his favourite band.
He ☹☹☹ [2] _____ _____ early.
He ☺☺☺ [3] _____ English, even in our French class!
I ☹ [4] _____ _____ my maths homework. Jack ☺ [5] _____ me.

 Use it!

4 Think of five sentences using *love*, *like*, *don't mind* and *hate*. Say your sentences to your partner. Do you agree?

> I don't mind cleaning the kitchen.   I hate doing it!

have got

I/you/we/they	he/she/it
We**'ve got** two new cameras.	She [1]**'s** got a new camera.
I [2] _____ **got** a plan of the school.	Alex **hasn't got** a plan of the school.
Have you **got** your own laptop? Yes, I [3] _____ . / No, I **haven't**.	[4] _____ he **got** his own laptop? Yes, he **has**. / No, he [5] _____ .

5 Complete the examples in the table above.

6 Complete the sentences with the correct form of *have got*.

1 Alex _hasn't got_ his own laptop. ✗
2 Alex _____ a tablet. ✓
3 They _____ a lot of laptops at coding club. ✓
4 Libby _____ her own computer. ✓
5 She _____ much free time. ✗

7 Complete the text with the correct form of *have got*. Then listen and check.
S.08

> We[1]_'ve got_ a new student in our class. Her name's Paola. What [2] _____ we _____ in common? A lot! She [3] _____ brown hair and blue eyes – just like me! [4] _____ she _____ any brothers and sisters? Yes, she [5] _____ . She [6] _____ two annoying little sisters, just like me. She [7] _____ any brothers. We [8] _____ the same trainers, phones and headphones! We both love playing table tennis. We [9] _____ any classes today because it's a holiday. I [10] _____ Paola's phone number, and I hope she's free to practise table tennis with me this afternoon.

 Use it!

8 Ask and answer questions using *have got*.

> Have you got any brothers or sisters?

WRITING
A personal profile

1 **Look at the photo. What does Ernesto like doing? Read his profile and check.**

1 Hi! 🏐 My name's Ernesto Mendes and I'm 14 years old. I'm from Vancouver in Canada. I live with my mum and dad, my grandma and my cat. My cat's name is Tiger 🐱. My best friends are Joel and Ruby.

2 My favourite free-time activity is gymnastics. I train every day. Training starts at 6am ⏰. It's tough, because I hate getting up early, but I love practising.

3 I also like going for bike rides on my own. I've got a new bike and I usually go for a bike ride after school. I haven't got much free time, but I always hang out with my friends at the weekend. We often go to Joel's place because he's got a swimming pool.

2 **Read Ernesto's profile again and answer the questions.**

1 Where is Ernesto from?
    He's from Vancouver in Canada.

2 Why does Ernesto get up early?
    _____

3 What does he like doing on his own?
    _____

4 What does he do at the weekend?
    _____

3 **Look at the *Useful language* box. Find and <u>underline</u> examples of apostrophes and commas in the profile. Match them with the correct use and write them in the box.**

Useful language

We use apostrophes:

• for contractions / short forms: *name's*
    _____

• to show possession: *My cat's name is Tiger.*
    _____

We use commas to indicate a pause:

I live with my mum and dad, my grandma and my cat.
    _____

4 **Rewrite the sentences with commas and apostrophes in the correct places.**

1 Were from South Africa.
    We're from South Africa.

2 Whats your history teachers name?
    _____

3 That isnt my tablet.
    _____

4 Ive got a cat three horses and a parrot!
    _____

5 My sisters friends very noisy!
    _____

Write your own personal profile.

PLAN

5 **Make notes for each paragraph.**

You, your family and friends
    _____

Your favourite free-time activity

• what it is and where you do it

• how often you do it
    _____

Other free-time activities

• what you like doing on your own or with friends

• when and where you do the activities

WRITE

6 **Write your profile. Remember to include three paragraphs, the information in Exercise 5, the present simple, adverbs of frequency, *love*, *etc*. + *-ing* and *have got*.**

CHECK

7 **Do you ...**

• describe you, your family and friends?

• explain your favourite free-time activity?

• say what other things you like doing, and when?

1

WHAT ARE YOU WATCHING?

LEARNING OUTCOMES
I can ...
- understand Tweets, a guided tour and a text about a Japanese film studio
- talk about TV shows and making movies
- write a description of my favourite internet or TV personality
- understand how to use the present continuous and present simple, and adverbs of manner
- ask for and give opinions
- use real examples, listen for specific information and understand new words.

Start it!

1 Look at the photo. What is the girl doing?
2 Before you watch, where do you watch TV shows?
3 What did John Logie Baird build? Watch and check.
4 How do you think TV changed the world?

Watch video 1.1

Language in action 1.2 p13

Language in action 1.3 p15

Everyday English 1.4 p16

Globetrotters 1.5 p18

VOCABULARY
TV shows

🎧 1.01 **1** Match eight of the TV shows in the box with the photos. Circle the four shows that aren't in the photos. Listen, check and repeat.

cartoon	☐	chat show	☐
comedy	☐	cookery show	☐
documentary	☐	drama	☐
game show	☐	on-demand series	☐
reality show	☐	soap opera	1
sports show	☐	the news	☐

2 Match the sentences with TV shows in Exercise 1.

1 'Put your potatoes in a pan and add some salt.'
  cookery show

2 'They're coming! We need to get out of here.'

3 'Giant pandas are in danger. There are only about 1,800 left.'

4 'We've got some really interesting guests on tonight's show.'

5 'Can they score in the last minute?'

6 'Today: Hurricane hits city.'

🎧 1.02 **3** Listen. Write the shows the people talk about.

1   *comedy*   4

2   5

3   6

🛡 LEARN TO LEARN

Using real examples

When you learn vocabulary, think of examples to help you remember it.

4 Think of an example of each type of TV show in Exercise 1.

💬 **5** Ask about your partner's TV shows. Can you guess what they are?

> *What type of show is it?*   *A sports show.*

💬 Use it!

6 Complete the sentences so they are true for you. Tell your partner.

1 I love watching _____.

2 My family often watches _____.

3 My favourite TV show is _____.

4 I hate _____.

Explore it! 🖱

Guess the correct answer.

Which country in the world watches the most TV?

a Poland   **b** USA   **c** Japan

Find an interesting fact about TV. Then write a question for your partner to answer.

READING

Tweets

1 Look at the pictures and titles. What do you think the Tweets are about?

2 Read the Tweets. Match the people with the TV shows.

1	Jack	a	a comedy
2	Holly	b	the news
3	Rory	c	an on-demand series

1.03

3 Write *J* (Jack), *H* (Holly) or *R* (Rory).

1 Who likes different TV shows from his/her friend? ____

2 Who does media studies? ____

3 Who is with his/her friend now? ____

4 Who talks about a friend in a different place? ____

4 Match the words with the definitions.

> average   episode
> season   subscribe

1 typical, normal _____

2 one individual show in a series _____

3 arrange to pay and receive something regularly _____

4 a period in which a show appears regularly on TV _____

 Voice it!

5 Imagine you are watching a famous event from history on the news. Discuss the questions.

1 Where are you?

2 Who or what can you see?

3 How many people are there?

4 How do you feel?

 Mad about TV @madabouttv
Apart from sleeping, the average teenager spends more time in front of a television than doing any other free-time activity! So … are you watching TV right now? Where are you watching it and who with? We want to know! Tweet us and send us your photos. #madaboutTV

 JackLong @JLo-o-o-ng
I'm learning about the history of TV in media studies this week. So for homework, I'm travelling back to 1969 to watch the news about Neil Armstrong, the first person on the moon.

 Mad about TV @madabouttv
@JLo-o-o-ng Amazing! Neil Armstrong and Buzz Aldrin are walking on the moon. 530 million people are watching them with you. We're over the moon too! #madaboutTV

 Holly Bardsley @HBards
At the moment, I'm sitting in my bedroom with my best friend @superfanz. We're watching our favourite on-demand series, *Stranger Things*, on my new tablet. We're super fans and this episode is soooooo scary! 👏

 Mad About TV @madabouttv
@HBards Here's a cool fact for you. More than 100 million people around the world subscribe to Netflix and you're one of them. Do you want to know about the next season of *Stranger Things*? 🤐 Just ask us! Spoiler alert! ❗ #madaboutTV

 Rory Green @RoryG
I'm waiting for my favourite comedy to start, so I'm taking a selfie and I'm messaging my friend @laughingboi 😊 at the same time! He isn't watching TV – he's listening to music. He doesn't like comedies.

 Mad about TV @madabouttv
@RoryG Believe it or not, if you're an average American teenager, you probably send about 128 instant messages a day! #madaboutTV

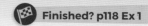 **Finished? p118 Ex 1**

LANGUAGE IN ACTION
Present continuous

Watch video 1.2
What are Ben and Nick doing?
What two things is the vlogger doing?

I	he/she/it	we/you/they
I'm sitting in my bedroom.	He¹'s___ **listening** to music.	Neil Armstrong and Buzz Aldrin ²_____ **walking** on the moon.
I'm not sitting in class.	He ³_____ **watching** TV.	We **aren't watching** the news.
Am I **listening** to music? Yes, I **am**. / No, **I'm not**.	**Is** Rory's friend **listening** to music? Yes, he **is**. / No, he **isn't**.	⁴_____ you **watching** TV right now? Where ⁵_____ you **watching** it?

> Pronunciation p141

⊙ Get it right!

We don't usually use some verbs with the present continuous. For example, *know, understand, like, love, prefer, remember.*

Do you understand me? **NOT** ~~Are you understanding me?~~

1 Complete the examples in the table above. Use the Tweets on page 12 to help you.

2 Write sentences with the present continuous.
1. Jack / watch TV / with 530 million other people.
   Jack is watching TV with 530 million other people.
2. Holly and her friend / not sit / in the library.
   _____
3. Holly and her friend / watch / an on-demand series now.
   _____
4. Rory / not watch / his favourite comedy at the moment.
   _____

3 Complete the blog with present continuous verbs.

This week I ¹*'m researching* (research) my favourite subject – TV! I'm very happy because I ²_____ (not do) it on my own. I ³_____ (prepare) a presentation with my friend Saul.

At the moment, Saul ⁴_____ (not talk) to me. He ⁵_____ (watch) a new online series and he ⁶_____ (make) notes. I'm tired right now, so I ⁷_____ (have) a break. But we ⁸_____ really _____ (enjoy) this project.

🎧 4 Complete the conversation with the present continuous form of the verbs. Then listen and check.
1.06

~~do~~	give	interview	not do
revise	ring	talk	watch

ROSA What ¹*are* you *doing* right now, Toni?
TONI I ²_____ to you.
ROSA Ha, ha. Very funny. ³_____ you _____ for the maths test?
TONI No, I ⁴_____ a chat show. Why ⁵_____ you _____ me?
ROSA Well, this maths homework ⁶_____ me problems. If you ⁷_____ anything important, can you help me?
TONI Sorry, Rosa. I can't talk now. They ⁸_____ _____ Ed Sheeran. I'll call you back, OK? Bye.
ROSA Great. Thanks a lot, Toni.

◔ Use it!

5 Write questions. Then discuss them with a partner.
1. what / you / wear?
   What are you wearing?
2. what / your teacher / do / right now?
   _____
3. where / your best friend / sit / today?
   _____

What are you wearing?	*I'm wearing …*

🎲 **Finished? p118 Ex 2**

VOCABULARY AND LISTENING
Making movies

1 Match the words with the people and things in the picture. Listen, check and repeat. 🎧 1.07

actor	☐	camera operator	☐
costume	☐	(digital) camera	☐
director	☐	lights	☐
make-up artist	☐	script	☐
set	☐1	sound engineer	☐

2 Circle the correct word in each sentence.
1 It's too dark. We need extra *lights* / *cameras*.
2 They're building the *director* / *set* this week.
3 We can't start filming – the main *operator* / *actor* isn't here.
4 Who is writing the *script* / *lights*?
5 I'm not wearing that *costume* / *camera*. No way!
6 We can't hear the voices very well. Where's the *make-up artist* / *sound engineer*?

🔵 Use it!

3 Choose a job in Exercise 1 and describe what you're doing. Can your partner guess the job?

> *I'm sitting in my chair. I'm talking to the actors and I'm looking at the set.*

A guided tour

4 Look at the photos. What are they? Where do you think you can see these things?

5 Listen and circle Matt's favourite film. 🎧 1.08
   a *Thor*   b *Avatar*   c *The Lord of the Rings*

🛡 LEARN TO LEARN

Listening for specific information
Check what type of answer you need (a number, a name, a place, a job, etc.) before you listen.

6 Read the questions in Exercise 7. Write the type of answer you think you need to listen for.

1	*a place*	4	_____
2	_____	5	_____
3	_____	6	_____

7 Listen again and answer the questions. 🎧 1.08
1 Where does Matt live? Wellington
2 How many people visit film locations in New Zealand each year? _____
3 What is Clara's job? _____
4 Where do the students go first? _____
5 How tall are some of the bigatures? _____
6 What is Martin's job? _____

🔵 Voice it!

8 What is on your dream film studio tour?

LANGUAGE IN ACTION
Present simple and present continuous

Watch video 1.3
What is he doing?
Describe two tips he gives.

Present simple	Present continuous
More than 3 million people ¹_____ locations for films here every year.	Today, I²_____ a film workshop with my media studies class.
Time expressions: *always, sometimes, never, every day/week*, etc.	Time expressions: (*right) now, at the moment, today, this morning*, etc.

1 **Complete the examples in the table above with the correct form of *visit*.**

2 **Circle the correct verbs.**
   1 Matt (*lives*)/ *is living* in Wellington.
   2 Matt and his class *wait / are waiting* for their tour guide.
   3 Martin *works / is working* hard today.
   4 Martin always *uses / is using* a digital camera.

🎧 1.09 3 **Complete the text with present simple or continuous verbs. Then listen and check.**

Media studies ¹ *is* (be) my favourite subject at school. I ² _____ (love) it! This week, we ³ _____ (study) the history of film. We ⁴ _____ (learn) all about talkies, CGI and lots more! I ⁵ _____ (not know) much about it. It ⁶ _____ (take) a long time and a lot of people to make a film.
Sorry! Time to go! My little brother ⁷ _____ (make) a lot of noise downstairs. I think he ⁸ _____ (watch) his favourite comedy with my mum and dad. They all ⁹ _____ (love) it and they always ¹⁰ _____ (laugh) a lot! 😄
What ¹¹ _____ you _____ (do) at school this week?

Use it!

4 **Rewrite the sentences with the verbs and time expressions. Use the correct tense.**

   do / sometimes   drive / now   ~~watch / always~~

   1 We / sports shows at the weekend..
      We always watch sports shows at the weekend.
   2 They / their homework together.
      _____
   3 My parents / me to sports club now.
      _____

Adverbs of manner

If I'm not explaining things ¹ *clearly* (clear), shout!
Talk ² _____ (quiet), please.
He's working ³ _____ (hard) today.

5 **Complete the examples in the table above with the correct form of the word in brackets.**

6 **Write the adverbs for adjectives 1–6. Circle the ones that don't use *-ly*.**
   1 nice   *nicely*   4 loud _____
   2 fast _____   5 happy _____
   3 beautiful _____   6 good _____

Use it!

7 **Write questions. Use the present simple or continuous and the adverb form of the word in brackets.**
   1 you always / make / new friends? (easy)
      Do you always make friends easily?
   2 you / speak / English / today? (good)
      _____
   3 your maths teacher / explain / everything? (clear)
      _____
   4 you / work / this term? (hard)
      _____

8 **Discuss the questions in Exercise 7.**

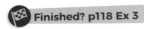 **Finished? p118 Ex 3**

SPEAKING
Asking for and giving opinions

🎧 **1** Listen to the conversation. Does Eva like the show?
1.10

EVA   What are you doing?

ALEX   I'm watching the second episode of this new comedy series.

EVA   But it's lunchtime.

ALEX   I'm not having lunch today. Lunch can wait.

EVA   So what [1] do you think of the show?

ALEX   I [2] _____ it! [3] _____ comedies?

EVA   No, I don't. I'm not [4] _____ them. I [5] _____ documentaries and dramas.

ALEX   Everyone's watching this one. It's really cool! Why don't you watch it with me?

EVA   I'm not sure.

ALEX   I think you'll really like it.

EVA   OK. Let's see.

ALEX   Well? What do you think of it?

EVA   Actually, it's [6] _____ !

🎧 **2** Complete the conversation with the phrases from the
1.10   *Useful language* box. Then listen and check.

Useful language

Do you like … ?

I like/love/hate/prefer watching …

I'm not really into it/them.

It's great/good/not bad/awful.

What do you think of … ?

3 Look at the *Everyday English* box. Find and <u>underline</u> the phrases in the conversation.

Watch video 1.4
Everyday English

Actually …   It's really cool!

Let's see.   Well?

4 Complete the conversations with the *Everyday English* phrases.

1   A   This actor is great, isn't he?

     B   _____ , I don't really like him.

2   A   _____ ? Do you like the show?

     B   Yes, I do. _____ !

3   A   Come with us to the gym on Saturday.

     B   Maybe, but I'm not sure. _____ .

PLAN

5 Write about some TV shows you want to talk about. Use the ideas below.

Which shows? _____

_____

What do you think about them? _____

_____

Why? _____

_____

SPEAK

6 Practise the conversation with your partner. Remember to use the present simple and present continuous, the vocabulary from this unit, and phrases from the *Useful language* and *Everyday English* boxes.

CHECK

7 Work with another pair. Listen to their conversation and complete the notes.

Which shows? _____

_____

What do they think about them? _____

_____

Why? _____

_____

WRITING
A description of a celebrity

1 **Look at the photo. What is the woman holding? Read the description and find the answer.**

2 **Match topics a–c with paragraphs 1–3.**
   a Why I like this person
   b An introduction to the person and her show
   c Typical episodes in the show

3 **Read Lidia's description again. Are the sentences *T* (true) or *F* (false)?**
   Rosanna Pansino …
   1 is from the USA. ____
   2 has a game show on the Internet. ____
   3 likes trying other people's recipes. ____
   4 makes unusual cakes. ____

4 **Find and <u>underline</u> examples of *but*, *and* and *or* in Lidia's description. Complete the *Useful language* box.**

> **Useful language**
>
> We use ¹_____ to add similar information.
> We use ²_____ to show different information.
> We use ³_____ when there is a choice of two or more things.

5 **Circle the correct word.**
   1 I don't like making cakes, *or* /(*but*)I love eating them!
   2 Ryan Higa is my favourite internet star *and* / *but* I often watch his videos.
   3 Do you prefer watching comedies *and* / *or* soap operas?
   4 Lots of people love chat shows, *and* / *but* I think they're boring.

My favourite internet star
By Lidia Suarez

1 ☐ Rosanna Pansino is my favourite internet star. She's an American actor, but she's also got a cookery show – *Nerdy Nummies*. She bakes fantastic cakes. I love the show and trying her recipes. She's got more than 10 million subscribers, and every month her show gets 75 million views.

2 ☐ In each episode, she explains how to make her cakes. But they aren't normal cakes! They're characters or objects from TV shows, video games, films or books. This week, she's making Batman cakes.

3 ☐ I like her because she's a great cook and because she makes the videos herself, too. She uses her own computer, camera and lights. She always explains her recipes clearly. They're easy to follow and the cakes taste great!

Write a description of your favourite internet or TV personality.

PLAN
6 **Make notes about these things.**
   1 Who the person is: _____
     What he/she does: _____
   2 What he/she does in each episode: _____
     _____
     What he/she is doing in this week's episode: _____
     _____
   3 Why I like this person and the show: _____
     _____

WRITE
7 **Write your description. Remember to include three paragraphs, the correct present tenses and adverbs, and *and*, *but* and *or*.**

CHECK
8 **Do you …**
   • use sentences with *and*, *but* and *or*?
   • give information about what the person usually does and is doing now?
   • explain why you like the person?

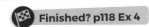 **Finished? p118 Ex 4**

AROUND THE WORLD

READING
An online article

1 Look at the photos. What kind of film can you see? What is happening in each photo?

🎧 2 Read the article and check your answers.
1.11

Globetrotters
Watch video 1.5
Indian cinema

- How many films does India produce a year?
- Where does the name Bollywood come from?
- How many different films can actors film at the same time?

Welcome to Studio Ghibli – the Japanese Disney!

Studio Ghibli is a Japanese animation studio in Tokyo. It produces films, TV adverts and series. The films look a bit like cartoons. They're exciting fantasy films and they tell stories about daily life. It can take up to eight years and thousands of hours to produce one film, so there's usually only one film a year. How do they do it?

First, someone thinks of an idea for a film and writers develop a script for the story. Then they think about the characters. What are the characters like? There are good and bad characters, and a lot of them are strong, independent girls. What do they look like? They've all got big eyes and colourful clothes, costumes and hair.

Next the script becomes a storyboard with all the drawings and frames for the film. In this photo, the artist is sketching each scene beautifully, frame by frame, on paper with a pencil. In the film *Ponyo*, there are 170,000 frames. Imagine that!

After that, the artists add colour to the characters and they draw the background for each frame.

The camera operator shoots each frame individually to show every movement that the characters make.

Next, actors record the dialogue, and the director checks the recording with the images. Finally, it's time to record the sound effects, background noises and theme music.

Do you like watching films? Why not try a Studio Ghibli film next time?

 **LEARN TO LEARN**

Understanding new words

Don't worry if you don't understand some words. First, try to get a general understanding of the article. Then guess the meaning of the new words.

3 Look at the highlighted words in the article. Try to guess their meaning. Then check in a dictionary.

- Look at the words before and after the word.
- Think of similar words in your language.
- Look at any pictures to help you understand.
- Look for other examples of the word in the article.

4 Think of your own sentences with the new words. Say each sentence, but don't say the new word. Can your partner guess it?

5 Read the article again. Put the steps in order.

a ☐ They prepare the storyboard.
b ☐ Actors prepare the words for the pictures.
c ☐1☐ A person thinks of an idea.
d ☐ They record all the sound.
e ☐ Artists add colour.
f ☐ A writer develops a script.

6 Read the article again. Answer the questions.

1 Where is Studio Ghibli?
_____

2 What does Studio Ghibli make?
_____

3 How long does it take to make a film?
_____

4 What are the characters like?
_____

5 What is special about the way they look?
_____

6 What do the artists use to create the storyboards?
_____

 Voice it!

7 Discuss the questions.

1 The directors, artists and camera operators in Studio Ghibli have a lot of patience. Why do they need patience?
2 Are you a patient person or not?

Explore it!

Guess the correct answer.

Spirited Away is a famous Studio Ghibli film. The location for the film is in …

a Taiwan. b Tokyo. c Seoul.

Find three more interesting facts about animated films. Choose your favourite fact and write a question for your partner.

VOCABULARY

1 The TV shows are wrong. Write the correct ones.

1 My little sister loves **soap operas**. Her favourite character is SpongeBob _____

2 That new **documentary** is so exciting, and it's only the second episode! _____

3 This **sports show** is about dolphins.
_____

4 Which guests are on the **soap opera** tonight?
_____

5 Only one person can win the car and the money in this **drama**. _____

2 Write the TV and film words for the definitions.

1 clothes that actors wear in films _____

2 a person who changes the actors' appearance
_____

3 the words for a film _____

4 the place where they film a TV show _____

5 the person who tells actors what to do _____

LANGUAGE IN ACTION

3 Complete the conversation with the present continuous form of the verbs.

HASAN   Hey, Yusuf. Are you at home?

YUSUF   Yes, I [1] _____ (watch) last night's music show. Where [2] _____ (you / call) from?

HASAN   I [3] _____ (stand) outside the house. I haven't got my keys.

YUSUF   Ring Mum.

HASAN   I [4] _____ (ring) you because Mum [5] _____ (not answer) her phone. Where are you?

YUSUF   I [6] _____ (sit) in the garden. The sun [7] _____ (shine), the birds [8] _____ (sing).

HASAN   Yusuf, can you let me in, please? NOW!

4 Complete the sentences with the present simple or present continuous.

1 The actor _____ the script at the moment. (not read)

2 _____ you usually _____ friends after school? (see)

3 The students _____ for their drama exam this week. (revise)

4 Simon always _____ TV after school. (watch)

5 Rewrite the sentences with adverbs of manner.

1 The children are talking in the library. (quiet)
_____

2 Are you writing in your notebooks? (careful)
_____

3 The teacher is explaining the activity. (clear)
_____

4 We're working for our exams. (hard)
_____

6 Complete Kim's blog with the present simple, present continuous and adverbs of manner.

My friend Ava often [1] _____ (come) to my place on Saturday afternoons and we [2] _____ (listen) to music together. This Saturday is different. My dad [3] _____ (drive) us to a film premiere. There's a lot of traffic, so we [4] _____ (not move) [5] _____ (quick). I usually [6] _____ (write) my blog on Saturday evening in my bedroom, but today I [7] _____ (type) it [8] _____ (slow) on my phone in the car!

LEARN TO LEARN

LEARN TO ... ORGANISE YOUR NOTEBOOK

When you organise your notebook, it helps you to study better.

1 Ask and answer with a partner.

1 What do you usually write in your notebook?
2 How often do you use your notebook when you study at home?
3 How can you organise your notebook better?

2 Look at Irina's notebook. Match the tips 1–5 with a–e.

1 Divide your notebook into sections so that you can find things quickly. ____
2 Use different colour pens for different things (for example, adjectives can be red, numbers can be green). ____
3 Highlight or underline important notes, words and facts. ____
4 When you write something, make a plan on the left and then write on the right. ____
5 Write all your homework notes (what page, what exercise) in the same place so that you don't forget what you have to do. ____

3 Look at the tips again. Complete the sentences.

1 Highlighting and underlining helps you see the _____ information.
2 You can use the _____ on the left when you're writing.
3 The _____ notes help you remember what to do at home.
4 You can use different colour pens for _____ things. It's your choice!
5 You can find notes quickly when you use different _____.

OWN IT!

4 Follow the plan to organise your notebook.

1 Divide your notebook into sections.
2 Choose different colour pens for your notes.
3 Get a highlighter pen for important information (or you can underline it instead).
4 Start using your notebook today!

5 Discuss with a partner. How can you keep your notebooks well all year?

---

notes | vocabulary | homework | grammar

Plan
Paragraph 1
El Rubius
Real name: Rubén Doblas Gundersen
The number 1 internet star in Spain
33 million subscribers
Paragraph 2
each episode: plays games, talks about funny things
this episode: He's chatting with some of his subscribers
Paragraph 3
Why I like him: He's funny, he always makes cool videos
Don't forget to use: and, or, but

My favourite internet star
by Irina Volkov
El Rubius is my favourite internet star, and the most popular internet star in Spain. He has more than 33 million subscribers. His real name is ...

2

OUT OF THE PAST

LEARNING OUTCOMES
I can ...
- understand texts about journeys and lives in the past
- ask and answer about the weekend
- write an account of a journey
- understand how to use the past simple, *there was/there were* and *a, an, some* and *any*
- talk about the weather and useful objects
- use word families and categorise vocabulary
- give feedback and design a museum display.

▶ Start it!

1 Look at the photo. Where are the people?
2 Before you watch, what do you know about the **ancient** Egyptians?
3 What did the Egyptians use to make boats? Watch and check.
4 Name three things you would like to see in Egypt.

Watch video 2.1

p25
Language in action 2.2

p27
Language in action 2.3

p28
Everyday English 2.4

VOCABULARY
The weather

🎧 **1** **What is the weather like in the photos? Circle the weather words that aren't in the photos. Listen, check and repeat.**
2.01

> cloudy   cold   ~~dry~~   foggy   ~~hot~~
> icy   rainy   snowy   stormy
> ~~sunny~~   warm   wet   windy

1 *dry, hot and sunny*
2 _____
3 _____
4 _____
5 _____

2 **Complete the sentences with adjectives in Exercise 1.**

1 It's _*cloudy*_ 🌥 today.
2 Is it _____ 🌡 all year?
3 August is usually _____ 🌧.
4 We love _____ 🌨 weather!
5 It isn't _____ ⛈. It's _____ 🌬.

🛡 **LEARN TO LEARN**

Word families (1)
Build your vocabulary by learning words from the same family. Many adjectives ending in *-y* come from a noun.

3 **Write the adjective forms.**

1 cloud   *cloudy*
2 fog   _____
3 ice   _____
4 rain   _____
5 snow   _____
6 storm   _____
7 sun   _____
8 wind   _____

💬 **Use it!**

4 **Complete the sentences with your own ideas. Tell your partner.**

1 When it's foggy, it's difficult to _____.
2 In hot, sunny weather, I always wear _____.
3 On wet days, I hate _____.
4 I think cold, snowy weather is _____.

Explore it! 🖱

Is the sentence *T* (true) or *F* (false)?

Snow isn't always white – sometimes there is pink snow in the Sierra Nevada mountains in the USA. ☐

Find an interesting fact about the weather. Then write a question for your partner to answer.

READING
Diary extracts

1 **Look at the photos. What do you think the girl is writing about?**

🎧 2 **Read the text. Check your answer to Exercise 1.**
2.02

3 **Read the text again and find these things:**
1 two American states _____
2 two types of furniture _____
3 five weather adjectives _____
_____
4 two musical instruments _____
5 two animals _____

4 **Match the highlighted words with the definitions.**
1 long trip to another place _____
2 wet and dirty after rain _____
3 a difficult task _____
4 not deep _____
5 vehicles with four wheels to transport heavy things _____
6 large animals like cows that can pull heavy things _____

5 **Complete the sentences with words from the text.**
1 People on the Oregon Trail were called _____ .
2 Oregon is on the _____ coast of the USA.
3 The adults and children didn't usually travel in the _____ .
4 Louisa travelled across the country with her _____ .
5 One of Louisa's brothers played the _____ .

 Voice it!

6 **Discuss the questions.**
1 Do you think diaries are important?
2 What challenges do you face each day?

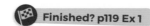 **Finished? p119 Ex 1**

The Oregon Trail

Between 1843 and 1869, more than 500,000 pioneers left their homes in the east of the USA to travel more than 3,000 km west to Oregon and California. Some people wanted to find gold and others wanted to start a new life.

The pioneers used wagons to cross the country. They took things like tables, chairs, tents and food – and also things they loved, like pianos! Oxen pulled the heavy wagons, but the adults and children usually walked or rode horses. The journey took between four and six months.

Louisa, age 14

Louisa Evans made the journey with her parents and two brothers, Samuel and Jesse. These are extracts from her diary.

8 April 1850
I got up at 5.30 am with mother and we made Johnny cakes for breakfast. Then we tidied the wagon and we left at 7 am. We didn't stop until 5 pm. After dinner, Samuel played his violin and we sang songs and danced. It was a warm, dry day and we travelled 24 km.

1 May 1850
Last night it was cold and rainy and all the tents got wet. I didn't sleep well and I felt tired all day. It wasn't easy to walk on the muddy ground. We didn't travel far today and we faced a new challenge: a river. It was high because of the rain and it looked dangerous. Did we manage to cross it? Yes, we did. We found a shallow part and walked across. We were lucky, but other people weren't.

LANGUAGE IN ACTION
Past simple

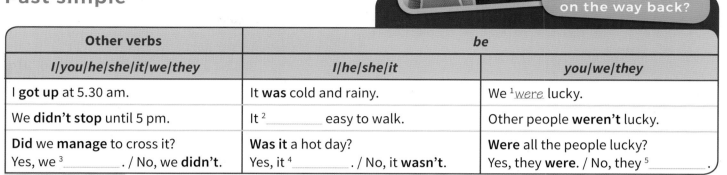

Watch video 2.2
How did she travel?
What happened on the way back?

Other verbs	be	
I/you/he/she/it/we/they	I/he/she/it	you/we/they
I **got up** at 5.30 am.	It **was** cold and rainy.	We ¹<u>were</u> lucky.
We **didn't stop** until 5 pm.	It ² _____ easy to walk.	Other people **weren't** lucky.
Did we **manage** to cross it? Yes, we ³ _____ . / No, we **didn't**.	**Was it** a hot day? Yes, it ⁴ _____ . / No, it **wasn't**.	**Were** all the people lucky? Yes, they **were**. / No, they ⁵ _____ .

> Pronunciation p141

1 **Complete the examples in the table above. Use the diary extract on page 24 to help you.**

2 **Rewrite the sentences in the past simple.**

1 More than 500,000 people leave the east coast.
   <u>More than 500,000 people left the east coast.</u>

2 The journey takes between four and six months.
   _____

3 On 8 April 1850, Louisa doesn't get up late.
   _____

4 8 April is a warm, dry day.
   _____

🎧 **3** **Complete the text with the past simple form of the verbs. Then listen and check.**
2.05

On 6 September 1620, 102 people ¹<u>left</u> (leave) England to travel 4,500 km to the USA. They ² _____ (not agree) with some of the religious views in Europe at that time, so they ³ _____ (decide) to start a new life.

They ⁴ _____ (travel) in a ship called the *Mayflower* and the journey ⁵ _____ (take) 66 days. The first half of the journey ⁶ _____ (go) well. Then the weather ⁷ _____ (change) and it ⁸ _____ (be) very cold and stormy. People became ill and some of them ⁹ _____ (not survive).

In December they ¹⁰ _____ (arrive) in Plymouth Bay. They ¹¹ _____ (not know) anything about this new land, but the local Wampanoag people ¹² _____ (help) them to find food and build houses.

💬 4 **Put the words in the correct order to make questions. Then ask and answer.**

1 last / your friends / you / see / Did / weekend / ?
   Did you see your friends last weekend?

2 you / did / after school / What / yesterday / do / ?
   _____

3 night / Were / asleep / at 10.30 pm / last / you / ?
   _____

4 any homework / your English teacher / Did / last week / give / you / ?
   _____

5 Was / hot / yesterday / the weather / ?
   _____

🔊 **Use it!**

5 **Think of questions to interview Louisa or a person from the *Mayflower* about their journey. Use the ideas below or your own.**

> the date   the weather   the food
> the other people   the challenges   new friends

6 **Take turns to ask and answer your questions.**

> *When did you leave?*

> *I left on 2 April with my family.*

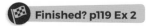
🏁 **Finished? p119 Ex 2**

VOCABULARY AND LISTENING
Useful objects

🎧 2.06 **1** Match the words with the pictures. Listen, check and repeat.

blanket	☐	bowl	☐	comb	☐
cup	☐	fork	☐	hairbrush	1
knife	☐	lamp	☐	mirror	☐
pillow	☐	plate	☐	scissors	☐
spoon	☐	toothbrush	☐		

1 2 3 4 5 6 7 8 9 10 11 12 13 14

🎧 2.07 **2** Listen. Write the objects the people are using.

1   toothbrush   4 _____

2 _____   5 _____

3 _____   6 _____

🛡 LEARN TO LEARN
Categorising

Recording new words in groups in your notebook can help you remember them.

3 Write words in Exercise 1 in the three groups. Can you add any more words?

Appearance	comb,
Bedtime	blanket,
Meals	bowl,

🔘 **Use it!**

4 Choose an object in Exercise 1. Ask questions to guess your partner's object.

> *Do you use it every day?*   *Yes, I do.*

A radio programme

🎧 2.08 **5** Listen to an interview about a discovery from the Bronze Age. What can you see in the photo?

🎧 2.08 **6** Listen again and correct the sentences.

1 Egtved is a small village in southern Germany.

    Egtved is a small village in southern Denmark.

2 The Egtved girl was 15 years old when she died.

_____

3 The girl died in the winter.

_____

4 She wore a shirt and trousers.

_____

LANGUAGE IN ACTION
there was/there were

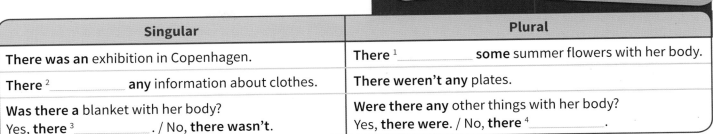

Watch video 2.3
Was the Viking Age peaceful?
Were there any coins in the exhibition?

Singular	Plural
There was an exhibition in Copenhagen.	**There** ¹_____ **some** summer flowers with her body.
There ²_____ **any** information about clothes.	**There weren't any** plates.
Was there a blanket with her body? Yes, **there** ³_____ . / No, **there wasn't**.	**Were there any** other things with her body? Yes, **there were**. / No, **there** ⁴_____ .

1 Complete the examples in the table above with *was, wasn't, were* or *weren't*.

◉ Get it right!

We use *some* and *any* with plural countable nouns and uncountable nouns.
some/any plates **NOT** ~~some plate~~
some/any information **NOT** ~~an information~~

2 Correct the sentences about the Egtved girl.

1 There wasn't an exhibition about the Egtved girl.
There was an exhibition about the Egtved girl.

2 There weren't any flowers with her body.
_____

3 There weren't any useful objects with her body.
_____

4 There was a hairbrush.
_____

5 There weren't a lot of travellers in northern Europe.
_____

💬 3 Ask and answer about the information in Exercise 2.

> *Was there was an exhibition about the Egtved girl?*

> *Yes, there was.*

4 Circle the correct words.

1 There were (some) / any students at the talk.
2 There was *an* / *some* interesting exhibition last week.
3 There weren't *some* / *any* audio guides.
4 Was there *some* / *any* snow in the mountains?
5 There wasn't *a* / *any* documentary on TV last night.

5 Complete the quiz with *was(n't)/were(n't)* and *a, an, some* or *any*. Then circle the correct answer.

DID YOU KNOW ...?

1 There *were* ✓ (some) / any humans in
? 250,000 years ago.
a Portugal (b Africa)

2 There _____ ✗ *a* / *an* alphabet with letters in **?** times.
a Aztec b Roman

3 There _____ ✓ *some* / *any* university courses for students in **?** in 1095.
a Paris b Oxford

4 There _____ ✗ *some* / *any* **?** for eating food in ancient Greece.
a forks b knives

5 There _____ ✓ *a* / *some* famous Roman **?** called Apicius.
a emperor b cook

🎧 6 Discuss your answers to the quiz. Then listen and check.
2.09

◉ Use it!

7 In pairs, choose a photo from Units 1 and 2 and look at it for one minute. Close your books. What can you remember?

> *Were there any clouds in the sky?*

> *Yes, there were. There were some white clouds.*

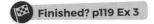 **Finished? p119 Ex 3**

SPEAKING
Talking about your weekend

🎧 **2.10** **1** Listen to the conversation.
Why was Andy in Wales?

CARLA	Hi Andy. ¹How was your weekend?
ANDY	² _____ OK, thanks.
CARLA	What ³ _____ ?
ANDY	I went to Wales for my grandad's 70th birthday.
CARLA	Cool! What ⁴ _____ like?
ANDY	It was cold, wet and windy.
CARLA	That's a shame. ⁵ _____ ?
ANDY	We stayed in a cottage.
CARLA	What was it like?
ANDY	Well, there wasn't any wi-fi and there were loads of noisy sheep outside.
CARLA	Really?
ANDY	Yes, really. In Wales there are about three million people and nearly ten million sheep.
CARLA	Wow. You learn something new every day!
ANDY	What ⁶ _____ ? What did you do?
CARLA	Nothing much. I watched TV and made some cakes.
ANDY	Sounds good!

🎧 **2.10** **2** Complete the conversation with the phrases from the *Useful language* box. Then listen and check.

Useful language

How was your weekend?

It was (OK/good/great/
amazing/awful), thanks.

What about you?

What did you do?

What was the weather like?

Where did you stay?

3 Look at the *Everyday English* box. Find and <u>underline</u> the phrases in the conversation.

Watch video 2.4
Everyday English

Nothing much.
Sounds good!
That's a shame.
You learn something new every day!

4 Which *Everyday English* phrase do we use to respond to … :

1 negative news? _____
2 interesting facts? _____
3 positive news? _____
4 a question? _____

PLAN

5 Write about something you did in the past. Use the ideas below.

Where you went: _____

What you did: _____

What the weather was like: _____

_____

Any problems you had: _____

_____

SPEAK

6 Practise the conversation with your partner. Remember to use the past simple and *there was/there were*, the vocabulary from this unit, and phrases from the *Useful language* and *Everyday English* boxes.

CHECK

7 Work with another pair. Listen to their conversation and complete the notes.

Where they went: _____

What they did: _____

What the weather was like: _____

_____

Any problems they had: _____

_____

WRITING
An account of a journey

1 **Look at the photos. Where do you think the man wanted to go? Read the account and check your answer.**

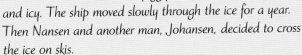

A difficult journey

Fridtjof Nansen was a Norwegian explorer. He wanted to be the first person to reach the North Pole. He set off on 24 June, 1893 from Oslo on a ship with 12 men.

At first, things went well, but by November, the weather was foggy and icy. The ship moved slowly through the ice for a year. Then Nansen and another man, Johansen, decided to cross the ice on skis.

The two men left the ship in March 1895, but there were a lot of problems. They couldn't reach the Pole and turned south.

The weather was warm, so the ice melted and it was difficult to travel. They built a shelter and waited there for eight months.

Finally, on 17 June, a British explorer found them. They arrived home safely on 13 August, 1896.

2 **Read the account again. Are the sentences *T* (true) or *F* (false)?**

1 Nansen left Norway in June 1893. ____
2 He started the journey on his own. ____
3 The weather was bad in November. ____
4 Nansen and Johansen didn't have any problems. ____
5 Nansen was the first person to reach the North Pole. ____
6 Nansen returned to Norway one year after he left. ____

3 **Read the phrases in the *Useful language* box. In what order are they in the account?**

Useful language

- ☐ At first, …
- ☐ Finally, …
- ☐ (He) set off on …
- ☐ There were a lot of problems.
- ☐ The weather was …

4 **Put the sentences in the correct order (1–5).**

a ☐ Finally, we arrived back safely at 9 pm.
b ☐ The weather was sunny but cold.
c ☐1☐ We set off from home early one morning.
d ☐ At first, we made good progress.
e ☐ There were a lot of problems that day.

Write an account of a journey.

PLAN

5 **Make notes for each paragraph.**

1 Who made the journey: _____
   When it started: _____
2 The first part of the journey: _____

   _____

   The weather: _____
3 How the journey continued: _____

   _____

   Any problems: _____
4 The end of the journey: _____

WRITE

6 **Write your account. Remember to include the past simple, *there was/there were* and phrases from the *Useful language* box.**

CHECK

7 **Do you …**
- use the past simple to talk about the past?
- explain what the journey was like?
- write your account in the correct order?

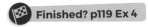
Finished? p119 Ex 4

THE HISTORY PROJECT

A museum display

💬 **1 Discuss the questions.**

1 What museums do you know?

2 What can you see in them?

3 What makes a museum interesting?

2 Read the texts. Then read the sentences and write S (scissors), M (mirror), L (lamp) or B (bowl).

1 The way of making this object is the same today as it was in the 1600s. S

2 It's black but you can see things in it. ____

3 Only rich people had objects like this. ____

4 This type of object first appeared in Egypt. ____

5 There was probably water in this. ____

6 This object had two uses. ____

7 It took a long time to find this object after a natural disaster. ____

8 This had connections with weather. ____

💬 **3 Which object is your favourite? Why?**

How to give feedback

🎧 **4 Read the tips about giving feedback. Then listen. Which objects do Sophie and Leo talk about?**
2.11

1 Read the piece of work.

2 Think about any areas that need improvement (the language, facts, organisation, design and photos, etc.).

3 Say what you like about the work.

4 Point out things that need improvement and make suggestions.

Sophie: _____   Leo: _____

🎧 **5 Listen again. Answer the questions.**
2.11

1 What did Sophie like about the display she read?

_____

2 What improvement did she suggest?

_____

3 What suggestions did Leo make?

_____

4 Do you agree with Sophie and Leo?

_____

5 What suggestions can you make to improve the displays?

_____

USEFUL OBJECTS DISPLAY

SCISSORS, STEEL AND IRON, 1628
Yi County, Anhui Province, China

This is one of the first pairs of scissors from Zhang Sijia's shop. Zhang Sijia opened the first scissors shop in China in 1628. He made all of the scissors by hand and followed the same 72 steps to make them. There is still a scissors factory in Hangzhou, China, and the workers use the same process as they did in the 1600s. The ancient Egyptians invented scissors, and today scissors are one of the most common objects in a home.

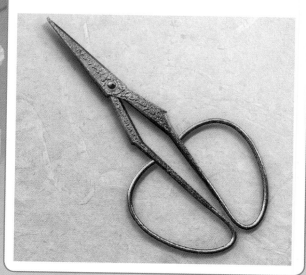

MIRROR, OBSIDIAN, AROUND 4000 BCE
Çatalhöyük, south-central Turkey

Archaeologists found this mirror in Çatalhöyük. It was one of the first cities in the world, and 8,000 people lived there. The mirror is made from a special black stone called obsidian, and it was one of the first mirrors in the world. People used these mirrors to look at themselves and also to look at the sun.

LAMP, BRONZE, CE 79
Pompeii, southern Italy

Archaeologists found this oil lamp in the city of Pompeii in 1752. It is in the shape of a dolphin. Bronze objects were expensive to make, so this lamp probably belonged to a rich family. Clay lamps were cheaper and more common. The city of Pompeii disappeared when the volcano Vesuvius erupted in the year CE 79.

TLALOC BOWL, TERRACOTTA, 3RD–8TH CENTURY
Veracruz, Mexico

This bowl probably held water. The face shows one of the faces of the Aztec figure Tlaloc, from ancient Central Mexico. People believed he sent good rain when he was happy to help plants grow, and he sent bad rain and storms when he was unhappy.

PLAN

6 Work in groups. Choose four historical objects. Then complete the steps below.

- Decide on the object that each student will research.
- Research your object and write a short text to use in the display.
- Find a photo or draw a picture of your object.
- Read each other's texts and give feedback.
- Make any changes or improvements.
- Work in your group and make your display.

PRESENT

7 Put your display on your classroom wall. Remember to follow the tips in *How to* give feedback and include correct facts, photos or pictures, and an attractive design.

CHECK

8 Look at your classmates' displays. Do they explain the four historical objects well? Give feedback to other groups on their displays.

VOCABULARY

1 Complete the sentences with the adjective form of the nouns in the box.

> cloud   fog   ice   rain   storm   wind

1 I don't like it when it's _____ because it's dark and noisy.

2 It's dangerous to drive when it's _____ and you can't see well.

3 Take an umbrella. It's very _____ today.

4 It's _____ outside. The trees are moving.

5 It's _____ today so we can't sunbathe.

6 Watch out! It's _____ outside. Don't slip.

2 Complete the sentences.

1 I need a _____ to stir my drink.

2 I've got a _____ so I can read in bed.

3 You can use a _____ or a _____ to make your hair look better.

4 Have you got any _____ to cut this paper?

5 I slept on my friend's sofa last night without a _____ or a _____ !

LANGUAGE IN ACTION

3 Complete the text with the past simple.

Meriwether Lewis [1]_____ (want) to explore more of the USA in the early 1800s. He and William Clark [2]_____ (leave) on 14 May, 1804 to go to the west of Mississippi. It [3]_____ (not be) an easy journey. They [4]_____ (meet) a lot of people, but they [5]_____ (not speak) their language. At times, they [6]_____ (not have) enough food and it [7]_____ (be) difficult to survive. After two years and more than 13,000 km, the men finally [8]_____ (complete) their journey in September 1806.

4 Complete the review with *there was(n't)* or *there were(n't)* and *a, an, some* or *any*.

I went to my local museum last week.

- 👍 [1]_____ amazing exhibition about Egypt.
- 👍 [2]_____ amazing things to see, like bronze mirrors and beautiful necklaces.
- 👍 [3]_____ board game called Senet. It was great fun to play.
- 👎 [4]_____ Egyptian mummies!
- 👎 [5]_____ café. I was hungry.
- [6]_____ good exhibitions in your town last week?

5 Complete the conversation with past simple verbs or *there was(n't)/there were(n't)*. Circle *a, an, some* or *any*.

CHLOE   What [1]_____ you _____ (do) at the weekend?

MAX   I [2]_____ (go) to my grandma's village. [3]_____ [4]*a / an* outdoor film festival.

CHLOE   Cool! [5]_____ you _____ (watch) [6]*some / any* films?

MAX   Yes, I [7]_____ . [8]_____ [9]*some / any* excellent films, but the weather [10]_____ (be) rainy.

CHLOE   Oh, dear. When [11]_____ you _____ (get) home?

MAX   This morning.

CHLOE   You [12]_____ (not message) me.

MAX   I know. [13]_____ [14]*some / any* wi-fi at home.

Self-assessment

I can use words to talk about the weather.	☹	😐	🙂
I can use words to talk about useful objects.	☹	😐	🙂
I can use the past simple.	☹	😐	🙂
I can use *there was/ there were*.	☹	😐	🙂

LEARN TO ... GUESS THE MEANING OF NEW WORDS

When you don't know a word, the beginning of a word, the end of a word and the rest of the sentence can help you guess the meaning.

1 Circle the answer that is true for you. Compare and discuss your answer with a partner.

When I see a word I don't know, I usually …

1 guess the meaning from the rest of the sentence.
2 see if I can understand part of the word.
3 ask the teacher what it means.
4 look in a dictionary.
5 write it in my notebook.

2 Read the text. Then tell your partner three things that surprise you.

Our incredible school trip!
By David North

Last February I went on a school trip to Wales.

The weather was very **unusual** for that time of year. Normally it's wet and windy, but it didn't rain once! It was a bit cold so we wore hoodies and trainers every day.

We **set off** very early on the first day, at about 5.15 am. The youth hostel in Wales was over 320 km away and it took nearly four hours. We couldn't take phones or tablets with us, so we chatted and played games instead.

When we saw the youth hostel for the first time, we were really happy. There was a small shop, and a room with table tennis and a TV. We hung out there in the evenings.

We did lots of **enjoyable** activities. We went rock climbing and sailing, and I tried windsurfing for the first time. My favourite activity was survival skills. We collected wood in the forest and then we built a small shelter. Clara and Ben saw some spiders and **ran away** – they hate things like spiders and bugs. In the evening, we cooked over a campfire. That night, we didn't sleep in the hostel. We slept in tents, and I shared a **tent** with my best friends.

It was an **unforgettable** experience and I was very sad to leave Wales.

OWN IT!

3 Read the text again. Discuss the questions about each of the words in bold with a partner. Make notes in your notebook.

1 Is it a noun, verb or adjective?
2 What clues about the meaning can you find in the text?
3 Does the word have a special beginning or end? What does it mean?
4 What do you think the word means?

4 Check the meanings of the words in a dictionary or with your teacher. Did the questions in Exercise 3 help you guess correctly?

> I think 'unusual' is an adjective.

> 'Unusual' describes the weather. The text says 'Normally it's wet and windy, but it didn't rain once!'

> Yes. It starts with 'un-' which means 'not'.

> I think 'unusual' means 'not usual'.

 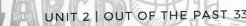

3

WHAT'S THE STORY?

LEARNING OUTCOMES
I can ...
- understand a fable and a traditional fairy tale
- tell an anecdote and express interest
- write a story
- understand how to use the past continuous and past simple
- talk about feelings and use prepositions of movement
- personalise sentences to remember new words, use my knowledge and use phrasal verbs.

▶ Start it!

1 Look at the photo. What is the boy doing?
2 Before you watch, what do you think people did in their free time in the past?
3 What did storytellers do? Watch and check.
4 What's your favourite story? Do you know where it came from?

Watch video 3.1

Language in action 3.2
p37

Language in action 3.3
p39

Everyday English 3.4
p40

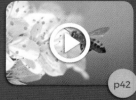

Globetrotters 3.5
p42

VOCABULARY
Adjectives of feeling

🎧 3.01 **1** Circle the adjectives to describe the people in the photos. Listen, check and repeat.

1 angry / bored

2 embarrassed / tired

3 surprised / worried

4 lonely / tired

5 afraid / upset

6 excited / nervous

> Pronunciation p141

2 Complete the sentences with adjectives in Exercise 1.

1 Sam's <u>afraid</u> of dogs so he doesn't want to walk through the park.
2 Bruno spoke to me today. I felt so _____. My face went red.
3 I'm _____ about my exams. What should I do?
4 It's Ana's birthday today! She's very _____.
5 I'm _____. This documentary isn't very interesting.

🛡️ LEARN TO LEARN
Personalising

You can write a sentence that is true for you to help you remember new words.

I often feel <u>tired</u> in the evening.

3 Write a personal sentence for six of the adjectives in Exercise 1.

1 _____
2 _____
3 _____
4 _____
5 _____
6 _____

💬 **4** Read your sentences to your partner, but don't say the adjectives. Can they guess the adjectives?

I feel … when I forget someone's name.

Embarrassed?

🔘 Use it!

5 Choose an adjective in Exercise 1 and tell your partner about a time when you felt like that. Ask questions to find out more.

I felt angry when my brother took my bike because he didn't ask me.

When did that happen?

Explore it! 🖱️

Guess the correct answer.

If you have didaskaleinophobia, you are afraid of …

a cheese.   b spiders.   c school.

Find out another unusual thing people are afraid of. Then write a question for your partner to answer.

READING
A fable

🗨 **1 Read the introduction and discuss the questions.**
1 What is special about fables?
2 Why do you think Aesop's stories are still important today?

Aesop's fables

Aesop was a writer from ancient Greece. He wrote a lot of short stories called fables. Fables usually have a moral message. The main characters are often animals, but they act like humans.

🎧 **2 Read the fable. Circle the best title.**
3.04
a The Fox's Dance   b The Monkey as King

One day, all the animals from the jungle were sitting in a circle. They were feeling excited because this was the day to choose their new king.

The animals took turns to give a speech about why they wanted to be king. When the fox was giving his speech, a lot of the other animals were getting bored, and they weren't listening. Then it was the monkey's turn, but he didn't give a speech. He danced, made silly faces and made the other animals laugh. They decided to make the monkey king.

The fox knew it was a bad decision, and he was angry. The monkey didn't have the right qualities to be a good king. He decided to play a trick on the monkey. 'I've got a present for you,' he told the monkey. 'Follow me.' The monkey followed him. All the animals were watching.

As they were walking through the jungle, the fox pointed towards a tree. 'Look at all those bananas!' he said. As the monkey was running to the tree, he fell into a trap. 'Help! Help!' he shouted. He wasn't dancing now.

'How can the monkey look after us and be our king?', asked the fox. 'He can't even look after himself.' The animals realised that they were wrong. 'You are our king now,' they told the fox. 'You are clever and you can protect us.'

3 Find words in the story that mean:
1 a place with a lot of trees _____
2 not serious _____
3 something that people give you on a special occasion _____
4 a hole in the ground to catch animals or people _____
5 to keep people safe _____

4 Answer the questions.
1 Why were the animals excited?
_____
_____
2 How did the other animals feel about the fox's speech?
_____
3 Why did the animals choose the monkey to be their king?
_____
4 What did the fox decide to do?
_____
5 What happened in the end?
_____
_____

 Voice it!

5 Discuss the questions.
1 What is the moral of the story?
2 What do you think a good leader needs?
3 Which other fables do you know?

🏁 **Finished? p120 Ex 1**

LANGUAGE IN ACTION
Past continuous: affirmative and negative

Watch video 3.2
Why was Sophia's first vlog bad? How many people follow her?

I/he/she/it	you/we/they
The fox ¹ _was_ **giving** his speech.	The animals ² _____ **sitting** in a circle.
He ³ _____ **dancing**.	They **weren't listening**.

1 **Complete the examples in the table above. Use the story on page 36 to help you.**

2 **Complete the sentences with was/were or wasn't/weren't.**

1 The animals weren't standing in a circle. They _were_ sitting.
2 The fox wasn't quiet. He _____ giving a speech.
3 The animals _____ watching each other. They were watching the fox and the monkey.
4 The monkey _____ walking to the tree. He was running.

🎧 3.05 3 **Complete the story with the past continuous form of the verbs. Then listen and check.**

One day, a hare ¹_was telling_ (tell) the other animals how fast he could run. At that moment, a tortoise ² _____ (walk) past. He heard the hare and he offered to race him.

The race began. At first, the hare ³ _____ (run) very fast and the tortoise ⁴ _____ (go) very slowly. The hare was soon near the end of the race. The other animals ⁵ _____ (not watch), so he decided to stop for a rest. He soon fell asleep. The tortoise continued to walk slowly while the hare ⁶ _____ (sleep). Just as the tortoise ⁷ _____ (finish) the race, the hare woke up. The other animals ⁸ _____ (shout) loudly – the tortoise was the winner!

The moral of the story is: don't be too sure that something is easy. Sometimes things are more difficult than you think.

4 **Complete the sentences with the past continuous form of the verbs in the box.**

make	not live	not work
~~read~~	take	travel	watch

1 At 9 pm last night, I _was reading_ a book.
2 Leo _____ selfies this morning.
3 Esma _____ a cake when I called.
4 My parents _____ at 10 pm last night. They _____ TV.
5 Sandra _____ at home this time last year. She _____ round the world!

🎧 **Use it!**

5 **Think of true sentences about things you were doing at these times. Use the activities in the box or your own ideas.**

at … o'clock yesterday morning/afternoon/evening
at … o'clock last Monday/Tuesday
this time two days/months/years ago
this time last week/month/year

chat to friends   do my homework   get up
go to bed   have breakfast/lunch/dinner
play basketball/computer games
walk home/to school   sleep

6 **Compare your sentences with a partner.**

At 8 o'clock yesterday morning, I was walking to school. What about you?

I wasn't walking to school. I was cleaning my teeth.

🎲 **Finished? p120 Ex 2**

VOCABULARY AND LISTENING
Prepositions of movement

Use it!

3.06 1 Match the prepositions with the pictures. Listen, check and repeat.

across	☐	along	☐	between	☐
down	[1]	into	☐	off	☐
out of	☐	over	☐	past	☐
through	☐	under	☐	up	☐

 1
 2
 3
 4
 5
 6
 7
 8
 9
 10
 11
 12

3.07 2 Circle the correct prepositions. Then listen and check.

1 Be careful! Don't fall *over* / *down* the stairs.
2 Who is that coming *out of* / *under* Bruno's house? Is it Carla?
3 Let's jump *into* / *up* the water together! Are you ready?
4 Don't cross the road *through* / *between* those cars. It's dangerous.
5 Why don't we swim *across* / *off* the lake to the other side? It isn't far.
6 Laura walked *along* / *past* me without saying hello.

3 In your notebook write about your journey to school today using the prepositions in Exercise 1. Compare with a partner.

First, I went out of my house. Then I walked along the road and over the bridge.

A radio phone-in

LEARN TO LEARN

Using your knowledge
Before you listen, think about what you already know on the topic and words you might hear.

4 Look at the photos and think about words you might hear.

3.08 5 Listen to Melissa's story. How many of your words in Exercise 4 do you hear?

3.08 6 Listen again and put the events in the correct order.

a ☐ A boy fell into the lake in the park.
b ☐ A photographer was taking a photo of Clayton's wife.
c ☐ Clayton and his wife were in a park.
d [1] Clayton Cook got married.
e ☐ Clayton jumped into the water and rescued the boy.
f ☐ Some children started shouting.

7 Close your books. Take turns to tell the story. Can you remember the events in order?

LANGUAGE IN ACTION
Past continuous: questions

Watch video 3.3
What were they doing in the country?
What was her sister holding?

I/he/she/it	you/we/they
Was he **wearing** his wedding clothes?	³_____ the children **standing** close to the lake?
Yes, he ¹_____ . / No, he ²_____ .	Yes, they ⁴_____ . / No, they **weren't**.

1 Complete the examples in the table above.

🎧 **2** Complete the dialogues with the past continuous
3.09 form of the verbs. Then listen and check.

1 A you / TV at 8 pm last night? (watch)
   <u>Were you watching TV at 8 pm last night?</u>
   B ✓ <u>Yes, I was.</u>

2 A What / your friends / at 7 am this morning? (do)
   _____
   _____
   B get up
   _____

3 A What / you / yesterday? (wear)
   _____
   _____
   B jeans and a hoodie
   _____

4 A your best friend / at 5 pm yesterday? (chat online)
   _____
   _____
   B ✗ play basketball
   _____

Past simple and past continuous

When Clayton **jumped** into the water, he ¹_____ (wear) his wedding clothes.
While the photographer ²_____ (prepare) his camera, Clayton **noticed** three children.

past simple
⟶
✗
past continuous

3 Complete the examples in the table above with the correct form of the word in brackets.

◉ Get it right!

We can use *when*, *while* and *as* + past continuous for a longer action in progress.

We use *when* + past simple for a shorter action that interrupts a longer one.

🎧 **4** Complete the text with the past simple or past
3.10 continuous. Then listen and check.

I ¹<u>was walking</u> (walk) to the bus stop one afternoon when I ²_____ (fall) over on the icy street.
I ³_____ (carry) a heavy bag with all my school things and I ⁴_____ (break) my glasses.
I ⁵_____ (feel) very embarrassed.
A lot of other people ⁶_____ (wait) for the bus, but they ⁷_____ (not help) me. However, one woman ⁸_____ (pick up) my bag and glasses and she ⁹_____ (find) an empty seat for me.
While I ¹⁰_____ (sit) there, she ¹¹_____ (clean) my face and gave me some water. But when I ¹²_____ (look) for her a few minutes later, there was no one there.

◯ Use it!

5 Work in pairs. Take turns to say a sentence to continue and finish the story below. Use the past simple and past continuous.

While I was walking to school this morning, I saw …

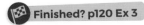 **Finished? p120 Ex 3**

SPEAKING
Telling an anecdote

🎧 3.11 **1** Listen to the conversation. Who is the story about and what was the person doing?

DAVID	[1]*Guess what happened* yesterday?
LAURA	No idea.
DAVID	Well, it didn't happen to me, [2]_____ Adrian.
LAURA	Go on.
DAVID	He was at the new shopping centre.
LAURA	You're kidding! [3]_____ a shopping centre? He hates shopping.
DAVID	He was looking for new trainers.
LAURA	[4]_____
DAVID	Yes, really. Now please stop interrupting. While he was looking at the trainers, someone bumped into him.
LAURA	Who was it?
DAVID	It was Neymar!
LAURA	No way! [5]_____
DAVID	I know.
LAURA	Did he take a photo?
DAVID	No, he didn't. He was too embarrassed. Can you believe it?
LAURA	What a great story!

🎧 3.11 **2** Complete the conversation with the phrases from the *Useful language* box. Then listen and check.

Useful language

Guess what happened (yesterday)?

It happened to …

Really?

That's amazing/incredible!

What was (he) doing (in) … ?

3 Look at the *Everyday English* box. Find and underline the phrases in the conversation.

**Watch video 3.4
Everyday English**

Go on.   No idea.   What a great story!
You're kidding!

4 Which *Everyday English* phrases do you use when you …
1 don't know? _____
2 hear something surprising? _____
3 want someone to continue? _____
4 liked a story that someone told you?
_____

PLAN

5 Write about something funny or unusual that happened. Use the ideas below.

Who did it happen to? _____

What was the person doing when it happened?

_____

What happened? _____

SPEAK

6 Practise the conversation with your partner. Remember to use the past simple and past continuous, the vocabulary from this unit, and phrases from the *Useful language* and *Everyday English* boxes.

CHECK

7 Work with another pair. Listen to their conversation and complete the notes.

Who the story happened to: _____

What the person was doing when it happened:

_____

What happened: _____

WRITING
A story

1 Look at the photo. What do you think Berat's story is about? Read the story and check your answers.

A funny story By Berat Demir

1 One night last summer, I was lying in bed when I heard a noise downstairs. At first, I thought it was our cat. I got up to see, but then I noticed my brother Eymen wasn't in his bedroom. I was worried.

2 I went downstairs. The front door was open, so I went out. I started walking down the road. A few minutes later, I saw Eymen. He was walking along the pavement on the other side of the road. He was wearing his bear pyjamas and he was carrying his teddy bear. Suddenly, he stopped. I ran towards him.

3 In the end, we walked back home together. Eymen was still sleeping. The next morning, he was very tired. When I asked him about the night before, he didn't remember it at all!

2 Read the story again and answer the questions.

1 When did the events happen?

2 Why did Berat go downstairs?

3 What did he do after that?

4 What was Eymen doing?

5 What happened the next morning?

3 Complete the sentences in the *Useful language* box with sequencing words and phrases from the story.

> **Useful language**
>
> 1 _____, I was lying in bed.
> 2 _____, I thought it was our cat.
> 3 _____, I saw Eymen.
> 4 _____, he stopped.
> 5 _____, we walked back home together.
> 6 _____, he was very tired.

Write a story.

PLAN

4 Think about a time when something interesting, funny or scary happened to you. Make notes about these things.

1 What was happening before the main events started: _____

   What happened first: _____

2 The main events of the story: _____

3 What happened in the end: _____

WRITE

5 Write your story. Remember to include three paragraphs, the past simple and past continuous, and the vocabulary from this unit.

CHECK

6 Do you ...
- use the phrases from the *Useful language* box?
- explain the main events?
- explain what happened in the end?

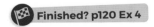 **Finished? p120 Ex 4**

AROUND THE WORLD

READING
A Turkish fairy tale

1 **Look at the pictures. What is happening in each picture? What do you think the story is about?**

🎧 3.12 2 **Read the fairy tale. Put the pictures in the order of the story.**

a ☐

b ☐

c ☐

3 **Find words in the fairy tale that mean:**
1 people who steal things
2 a very big and frightening creature
3 very afraid
4 not alive
5 a white bird
6 something that gives information

Globetrotters
Watch video 3.5
A bee's story

- Where are bees very busy?
- What is honey used for?
- Who did artists in the 18th century paint?

4 **Read the fairy tale again. Answer the questions.**
1 Why did the boy start his journey?

_____

2 How did he feel when he started the journey?

_____

3 What did the ogre try to do?

_____

4 Why do you think he felt afraid at the end?

_____

The boy who found fear

Once upon a time, a woman and her son lived in a small house in a forest. They didn't have any neighbours, and the lonely boy stayed at home with his mother every day.

One winter's evening, they were having dinner when a storm started. The wind blew the door open and the mother said, 'Close the door. I feel fear.'

'What is fear?' asked the boy.

'Fear is when you feel afraid,' she replied.

'I don't understand. I want to find fear.'

So the next morning, the boy set off confidently. While he was looking for fear, he met a lot of different people and he faced a lot of challenges. First, there was a group of robbers. They made him do dangerous and difficult things, but he wasn't afraid. He continued his journey.

LEARN TO LEARN

Phrasal verbs

A phrasal verb is a verb + a small word like *for* or *on*. They have a special meaning which is different from the verb on its own.

5 Find phrasal verbs in the story that mean:

1 to start a journey _____
2 to try to find _____
3 to find by accident _____
4 to arrive or reach _____
5 to continue _____

6 Complete the sentences with the phrasal verbs in Exercise 5.

1 Are we all ready to go? Let's _____ now before it gets too hot.

2 A I don't think it's a good idea to _____ in the dark.

  B OK. Let's camp here for the night.

3 Can you help me _____ my phone?

4 A How long did it take you to _____ the beach?

  B Ages! It was quite far away.

5 While I was doing some research, I _____ this photo of our street in 1885.

7 Think of your own sentences with the phrasal verbs in Exercise 5. Say your sentences but don't say the phrasal verb. Can your partner guess it?

Voice it!

8 Answer the questions.

1 When does the boy show fear? Why?

2 Is fear a positive or a negative quality?

3 Is everybody always afraid of the same things?

Explore it!

Is the sentence *T* (true) or *F* (false)?

The story of *Cinderella* first appeared in a Chinese book around the year 850. ☐

Find another interesting fact about a fairy tale. Write a question for your partner to answer.

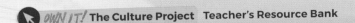
OWN IT! The Culture Project   Teacher's Resource Bank

Next, he came across an angry ogre who tried to attack him, but the boy ran away. After that, he got to the sea. There was a terrible storm and he saw a ship in great danger. The people on the ship were terrified and they were shouting for help, so he jumped into the water and saved them. He wasn't afraid at all.

He went on until finally he got to a city. There were people everywhere and it was very busy. One man told the boy that the people were sad because their king was dead, but today they were choosing a new king. Just then, three beautiful doves flew down from a tower and they sat on the boy's head. The people were excited. 'This is the sign! You are our king!'

At that moment, he saw into the future: he was the king, he was trying to make everyone happy, but the people were angry. And he suddenly realised what fear was, and he was afraid.

3 REVIEW

VOCABULARY

1 Complete the sentences with the adjectives.

> afraid   embarrassed   surprised   tired   upset

1 Elsa looks _____ and she's crying.
2 I can't believe I won! I'm really _____ .
3 My dad is _____ of heights. He can't go up tall buildings.
4 I forgot my friend's birthday. I was so _____ !
5 I'm really _____ . I didn't sleep much.

2 Complete the story with the prepositions.

> across   between   down   into
> out of   through   under   up

Tiger the cat went ¹_____ the front door and walked ²_____ two cars ³_____ the road. He went ⁴_____ the park and climbed ⁵_____ a tree. Then a mouse appeared. 'Lunch!' thought Tiger. He climbed ⁶_____ the tree and followed it. The mouse ran ⁷_____ the grass and then disappeared ⁸_____ a stone. 'Maybe I'll have lunch at home today,' said Tiger.

LANGUAGE IN ACTION

3 What was happening at 10.30 am yesterday? Write two sentences in the past continuous.

1 it / not snow – rain
_____
2 I / not study – chat / with my friends
_____
3 Alex / not read / a book – listen / to music
_____
4 Eva and Helen / not talk – have / a snack
_____

4 Write past continuous questions. Then match them with the answers (a–d).

1 you / wear / jeans / yesterday? ___
_____
2 Lidia / work / at 10 pm last night? ___
_____
3 where / we / go / last Saturday at 7 pm? ___
_____
4 what / Ollie and Brad / do / an hour ago? ___
_____

a We were going to the cinema.
b Yes, she was.
c They were taking photos.
d Yes, I was.

5 Complete the text with the past simple or past continuous form of the verbs.

Beth ¹_____ (study) at school when she ²_____ (write) her first novel. She ³_____ (post) her book online while she ⁴_____ (sit) in her bedroom at home. She soon ⁵_____ (discover) that lots of young people ⁶_____ (read) her story. Two years later, it had 19 million reads on the website and it ⁷_____ (win) a prize for teen fiction. When Beth ⁸_____ (leave) school, she ⁹_____ (go) to university. She ¹⁰_____ (complete) two more books while she ¹¹_____ (do) a physics course, and a TV company ¹²_____ (make) her first novel into a film in 2018.

Self-assessment

I can use adjectives to talk about feelings.	☹ ☺ ☺
I can use prepositions to talk about movement.	☹ ☺ ☺
I can use the past continuous to make affirmative and negative sentences and questions.	☹ ☹ ☺
I can use the past simple and the past continuous.	☹ ☺ ☺

LEARN TO ... GUESS THE MEANING OF NEW WORDS

You can help your partner learn vocabulary by writing sentences with missing words for them to guess.

1 Elif writes sentences with missing words for a friend to guess. Can you guess what the words are? Discuss with a partner.

> OK, the first one. Is it an adjective?

> Yes, it is.

> Is it 'happy'?

> No. Try again!

1 I was _____ because my football team were winning.

2 The plane flew _____ the city.

3 The boy felt _____ when he called his teacher 'mum'.

OWN IT!

2 Choose five words from the box. Write five sentences with missing words like the sentences in Exercise 1.

> between bored jungle nervous protect
> surprised tired trap under worried

1

2

3

4

5

3 Show your sentences to your partner. Can they guess the missing words?

4 Why is it a good idea to learn words in sentences? Discuss with your partner.

5 Close your book. Take turns to say the five words you chose in Exercise 2. Can your partner remember your sentences?

> The word was 'bored'. What was the sentence?

> 'I feel bored when ... .' No, sorry, can you help me?

> OK. It starts, 'I was bored because ...'.

> I remember! 'I was bored because ... '.

4

THE BEST THINGS IN LIFE ARE FREE

LEARNING OUTCOMES

I can …

- understand texts about money and caring jobs
- make and respond to requests
- write an opinion essay
- understand how to use *could*, comparative and superlative adjectives, *too*, *too much*, *too many* and *(not) enough* + noun
- talk about money and caring jobs
- remember words with similar meanings and listen for key words
- reach agreement as a group and make a poster.

▶ Start it!

1 Look at the photo. How are the girls feeling?

2 Before you watch, how do you help other people?

3 How do you feel when you help? Watch and check.

4 Which of the ways of helping in the video do you like best?

Watch video 4.1

p49

Language in action 4.2

p51

Language in action 4.3

p52

Everyday English 4.4

VOCABULARY
Money verbs

1 Look at the verbs in the box. Then match the sentences with the photos.

> borrow change cost earn lend
> owe pay save sell spend

1 Don't worry. I can **pay** for you, too. _g_
2 Don't **spend** your money on more video games. **Save** it for something you need. ___
3 Friendships don't **cost** money. They're free! ___
4 I want to **earn** money. Can I wash your car? ___
5 I **owe** my friend £50. I can **sell** my bike. ___
6 **A** Could you **lend** me some money? ___
  B How much do you want to **borrow**? ___
7 I want to **change** this money, please. ___

🎧 **2** Listen to the verbs in Exercise 1 and repeat.
4.01

🎧 **3** Listen and write the correct verb from Exercise 1 for each situation. Sometimes there is more than one possible answer.
4.02

1 ____pay____   4 _____
2 _____   5 _____
3 _____

🛡 LEARN TO LEARN
Similar words
Many words have similar meanings. Think of ways to help you understand the differences.

> You <u>lend</u> money to someone (it's yours).
> You <u>borrow</u> money from someone (it isn't yours).

4 Look at these pairs of verbs. Think of more ways to remember the different meanings.
  spend / buy   earn / win

🗣 **5** Compare with a partner. How does your partner remember the meanings?

🔘 **Use it!**

6 Complete the sentences with your own ideas. Tell your partner.
1 A good way to earn money is to _____
  _____
2 The last time I borrowed money was _____
  _____
3 I spend most of my money on _____
  _____

Explore it! 🖰

Is the sentence *T* (true) or *F* (false)?

In Zimbabwe, there was a $100 trillion banknote. At that time, bread cost $300 billion. ☐

$3,000,000,000

Find another interesting fact about money. Then write a question for your partner.

READING
A newspaper article

1 **Look at the photos. What do you think the man did?**

2 **Skim the article and choose the correct summary.**

a A man sold his home and bought a caravan to travel around the world for three years.

b A man lived without money for three years.

🎧 3 **Read the article and answer the questions.**
4.03

1 Where did Mark live after he sold his own home?

_____

2 How did he use his laptop without electricity?

_____

3 Which three things were difficult for him at first?

_____

4 What did he buy after his time without money?

_____

🎤 **Voice it!**

4 **Imagine you can interview Mark Boyle after his three years without money. Write questions to ask him using the ideas below.**

Family and friends: _____

_____

Clothes: _____

_____

Food: _____

_____

Work: _____

_____

Travel: _____

5 **Take turns to be Mark Boyle and the interviewer and do the interview.**

How often did you see your family?

When did you see your friends?

A different life

Can you imagine living for a day without money?
Mark Boyle, from Ireland, did that for three years.

Mark had a good job and he earned a lot of money. One day, a friend challenged him to live without money. Mark decided he could change his life and do it.

First, he sold his houseboat, and he went to live in a caravan on a farm. He kept his laptop and mobile – he knew he could use solar power to charge them. He couldn't make any calls, but he could receive them.

The first few months were the worst – simple things were more difficult than before. Mark couldn't buy food, have a shower or travel easily. But he soon found his own food – usually vegetables, fruit and other plants. He made a stove to cook outside and he collected wood to use as fuel. He washed in a river and he used plants to clean himself. He even made his own toothpaste! He walked or cycled everywhere, so he was fitter and healthier than he was before.

So, was life without money better for Mark than life with money? Yes, it was. He was happier than before, and the best thing was that he felt more alive. He also discovered that friendship is more important than money.

The biggest and most difficult decision for Mark was returning to a life with money. After three years without money, what was the first thing he bought? A pair of trainers from a charity shop!

🏁 **Finished? p121 Ex 1**

LANGUAGE IN ACTION
could

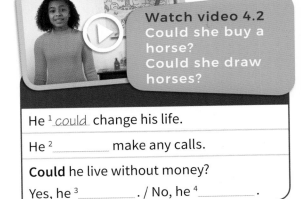

Watch video 4.2
Could she buy a horse?
Could she draw horses?

He ¹ _could_ change his life.	
He ² _____ make any calls.	
Could he live without money?	
Yes, he ³ _____ . / No, he ⁴ _____ .	

1 Complete the examples in the table above. Use the article on page 48 to help you.

2 Complete the sentences with *could* or *couldn't* and the verbs in brackets. Check your answers in the article.

  1 Mark _could receive_ calls on his phone. (receive)

  2 He _____ food. (buy)

  3 He _____ his laptop with solar power. (charge)

  4 He _____ a shower. (have)

Use it!

3 Complete the sentences. Use *could/couldn't* and the ideas in the box.

> buy my own clothes
> make my own lunch
> ride a bike   use a laptop

  1 When I was five, I _____ .

  2 When my grandparents were young, they _____ .

  3 A year ago, I _____ .

4 Ask and answer with a partner.

> *Could you buy your own clothes when you were five?*

Comparative and superlative adjectives

	Adjective	Comparative	Superlative
Short adjective	fit	¹ _fitter_	the fittest
	happy	² _____	the happiest
Long adjective	important	³ _____	the most important
	difficult	⁴ _____	the most difficult
Irregular adjective	good	⁵ _____	the best
	bad	worse	⁶ _____

5 Complete the examples in the table above. Use the article on page 48 to help you.

Get it right!

We use *than*, not *that*, to compare two things.
My sister is fitter than me. **NOT** ~~My sister is fitter that me.~~

6 Complete the sentences with the comparative or superlative form of the adjectives.

  1 Life for Mark without money was _better_ (good) than before.

  2 _____ (good) thing was that he felt more alive.

  3 _____ (difficult) decision was to return to a life with money.

🎧 4.04   7 Complete the text with the comparative or superlative form of the adjectives. Then listen and check.

> It's the fourth Friday in November and it's Black Friday. It's ¹_the busiest_ (busy) shopping day of the year. Things are ² _____ (cheap) than usual today. Shoppers can get ³ _____ (good) prices for ⁴ _____ (late) gadgets or ⁵ _____ (stylish) trainers. In my opinion, Black Friday is ⁶ _____ (bad) day of the year. People seem to be ⁷ _____ (interested) in shopping than anything else! I think we could all be ⁸ _____ (happy) people without spending money all the time.

Use it!

8 Choose a topic from the box or use your own. Discuss with a partner. Use comparatives and superlatives.

> maths / history / science
> market / shopping centre / online shopping

History is more difficult than … but … is the most difficult.

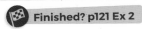 **Finished? p121 Ex 2**

VOCABULARY AND LISTENING
Caring jobs

🎧 **1** Match eight jobs with the photos. Circle the jobs
4.05   that aren't in the photos. Listen, check
        and repeat.

carer	☐	charity worker	☐
firefighter	☐	lawyer	☐
lifeguard	☐	nurse	☐
paramedic	☐	police officer	☐
refuse collector	☐	surgeon	☐
vet	☐1☐	volunteer	☐

> Pronunciation p141

2 Write which person you need in these situations.

1 You're at the swimming pool. Your friend has a
   problem. _lifeguard_

2 There's a fire at your school. _____

3 Your grandma needs help at home. _____

4 Your cat has a problem with its eye. _____

5 Your friend is in hospital. This person is doing
   an operation on them. _____

🔊 **Use it!**

3 Work with a partner. Discuss the questions.

1 What do the jobs in Exercise 1 have in common?

2 Which people in these jobs do you see every week?

3 Which job would you like to do?

Monologues

💬 **4** What do you think are the best and worst things
       about doing a caring job? Discuss with a partner.

🎧 **5** Listen and match the speakers with their jobs.
4.08   There is one extra job.

Speaker 1 ____	a lifeguard	d nurse
Speaker 2 ____	b paramedic	e vet
Speaker 3 ____	c volunteer	
Speaker 4 ____		

🛡 LEARN TO LEARN

Identifying key information
When you are matching people with information, check
key words before you listen. This helps you to focus on
the information you need.

6 Read the questions in Exercise 7. Circle the key
     words you need to listen for.

🎧 **7** Listen again. Write *1*, *2*, *3* or *4*.
4.08   Who …

a studies and works? ____

b doesn't have a job now? ____

c sometimes doesn't have lunch? ____

d was bored in their old job? ____

e sells things that help other people? ____

f enjoys making people feel happier? ____

💬 **8** Imagine a day in the life of one of the people in
       the jobs in Exercise 1. Write five sentences about
       your day in your notebook. Read your sentences
       but don't say the job. Can your partner guess?

> *I sometimes work all night.*

> *Is it a nurse?*

LANGUAGE IN ACTION
too, too much, too many

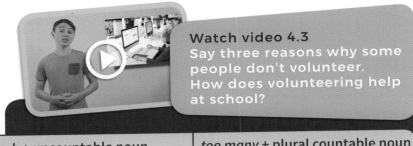

Watch video 4.3
Say three reasons why some people don't volunteer. How does volunteering help at school?

too + adjective	too much + uncountable noun	too many + plural countable noun
I'm **too** ¹_____ to have lunch.	Lots of people have got **too much** ²_____.	We've all got **too many** ³_____.

1 **Complete the examples in the table above with the words in the box.**

> busy   clothes   work

2 **Read the sentences about the people you listened to on page 50. Circle the correct words.**

1 The hours were (too) / too much / too many long in the paramedic's last job.

2 The volunteer thinks people own too / too much / too many books.

3 Sometimes the pool is too / too much / too many noisy for the lifeguard.

4 The vet spends too / too much / too many time at work.

3 **Complete the questionnaire with too, too much or too many.**

All about you!

Have you got ...

1 _too much_ homework this week?

2 _____ clothes?

Do you ...

3 spend _____ money on clothes?

4 buy _____ sweets?

Are you ...

5 _____ busy to listen to your friends?

6 _____ young to drive a car?

 Use it!

4 **Work with a partner. Ask and answer the questions in Exercise 3.**

(not) enough + noun

I've got ¹_____ (time).	I don't have ²_____ (money).

5 **Complete the examples in the table above with the words in brackets and enough.**

🎧 6 **Complete the text with the words in the box. Then listen and check.**
4.09

> enough chairs   enough space   enough time
> too far   too many animals   too many people
> too much information   too noisy   ~~too young~~

I'm ¹_too young_ to have a full-time job, but every Saturday I'm a volunteer with a local vet. I cycle there because it isn't ²_____ from my house. I help the receptionist when she hasn't got ³_____ to do everything. Last week, there were ⁴_____ in the waiting room — we didn't have ⁵_____ for them to sit on! Sometimes it gets ⁶_____ for me, especially when there are ⁷_____ and there isn't ⁸_____ in the waiting room.
The best thing: I love animals and I can spend all day with them! ☺
The worst thing: Sometimes there's ⁹_____ for me and I don't understand it all.

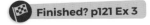 **Use it!**

7 **Imagine a day doing your dream job. Make notes. Then compare with a partner.**

- What the job is: _____
- The best thing: _____
- The worst thing: _____

> *My dream job is to be a firefighter. It's an exciting job, but it can be dangerous.*

🎲 **Finished? p121 Ex 3**

SPEAKING
Making requests

🎧 4.10 **1** Listen to the conversation. Who lends Rita some money?

BILLY   RITA   GREG

BILLY   Hey, Rita. What's up? You look a bit worried.

RITA   I am. ¹ *Could you do me a favour* ?

BILLY   ² _____ . What do you need?

RITA   ³ _____ lending me £10?

BILLY   Ah. ⁴ _____ . I spent too much money at the weekend.

RITA   OK, no worries. What about you, Greg?

GREG   Maybe. What's it for?

RITA   I want to buy a bag for Maisie's birthday. There's a really cute one that I want to get her, but I haven't got enough money.

GREG   When's her birthday?

RITA   Yesterday! Please, Greg.

GREG   ⁵ _____ , since you asked so nicely. There you are.

RITA   Thanks, Greg. You're the best! I owe you one.

GREG   Actually, you owe me ten!

🎧 4.10 **2** Complete the conversation with the phrases from the *Useful language* box. Then listen and check.

> **Useful language**
>
> Could you do me a favour?
>
> I'm sorry, I can't.
>
> It depends.
>
> Sure.
>
> Would you mind … + -ing … ?

3 Look at the *Everyday English* box. Find and <u>underline</u> the phrases in the conversation.

> **Watch video 4.4**
> **Everyday English**
>
> cute   I owe you one.
>
> There you are.   What's up?

4 Complete the conversations with the *Everyday English* phrases.

   1   A   _____ Kate?

        B   I need a favour.

   2   A   Thanks for paying. _____ .

        B   Any time.

   3   A   Can I borrow your phone for a second?

        B   Sure. _____ .

   4   Look at that little dog! It's so _____ .

> ## PLAN
>
> **5** Work in groups of three. One person wants to borrow something. One friend can't lend it, but the other can. Make notes.
>
> What the person wants to borrow and why:
>
> _____
>
> Why one friend can't lend it:
>
> _____
>
> ## SPEAK
>
> **6** Practise the conversation in your groups. Remember to use *(not) enough* and *too, too much*, *too many*, the vocabulary from this unit, and phrases from the *Useful language* and *Everyday English* boxes.
>
> ## CHECK
>
> **7** Work with another group. Listen to their conversation and complete the notes.
>
> What the person wanted to borrow and why:
>
> _____
>
> _____
>
> Why one friend couldn't lend it: _____
>
> _____

WRITING
An opinion essay

1 Read Min-Seo's essay. Does she agree with the statement?

> ### Professional sports stars earn too much money. Do you agree?

By Min-Seo Lim

1 Nowadays, sports stars can earn a lot of money. Some basketball players earn more than $40 million every year. In my opinion, this is too much.

2 First of all, sports stars work less than other people. They only entertain people for a short time each week. Also, they have long holidays.

3 Personally, I think that other jobs are more important. For example, nurses, like my dad, save lives. I also think it's easier to live without sport or sports stars than to live without nurses and firefighters.

4 To sum up, I believe that some sports stars earn too much money and people with important life-saving jobs don't earn enough. We need to find a better and fairer way to pay those people more.

2 Circle the correct words.

1 According to Min-Seo, sports stars earn *enough / too much* money.
2 Min-Seo thinks sports stars *help / entertain* people.
3 In Min-Seo's opinion, sports stars have got *more / less* important jobs than firefighters.
4 It is *easier / more difficult* to live without nurses than without sports stars.
5 People with life-saving jobs don't *earn enough / earn too much* money.

3 Complete the phrases in the *Useful language* box.

> **Useful language**
>
> ¹ _____ opinion   ² _____ of all
> ³ _____ , I think that   ⁴To _____ up
> ⁵I _____ that

4 Put the words in the correct order.

1 need / less / think / Personally, / we / homework / I / that _____

2 students / homework / In / too much / have / opinion, / my _____

3 work / all, / enough / in class / do / we / of / First _____

> Write your own opinion essay.
>
> ## PLAN
>
> **5** Choose one of these topics. Make notes about the information you need for each paragraph.
> - Pop stars earn too much money.
> - Money can't buy happiness.
>   1 Introduce the topic and give your opinion
>   2 Give a reason for your opinion
>   3 Give a second reason
>   4 Summarise your opinion
>
> ## WRITE
>
> **6** Write your opinion essay. Remember to include (*not*) *enough* and *too, too much, too many*, and phrases from the *Useful language* box.
>
> ## CHECK
>
> **7** Do you ...
> - have four paragraphs?
> - give reasons for your opinions?
> - summarise your opinion at the end?

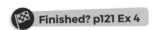
Finished? p121 Ex 4

THE SOCIAL STUDIES PROJECT

A poster

1 **What is the purpose of the poster? Read and check.**

   a   to encourage more people to use a local park
   b   to ask for more volunteers to clean the park
   c   to tell people about a charity event

2 **Read the poster again. Under which heading can you find this information?**

   1   the place for the activity   _Where?_
   2   the type of activity _____
   3   the people organising the activity _____
   4   the reasons why it is a useful thing to do _____
   5   the time and place to meet _____
   6   why volunteers enjoy the activity _____

How to agree as a group

3 **Read the tips on how to agree as a group. Put them in the best order.**

   a ☐ Ask other people for their opinions.
   b ☐ Make a decision as a group. Check everyone agrees.
   c ☐ Introduce the decision you need to make.
   d ☐ Give your own opinion politely.
   e ☐ Interrupt politely if you want to comment.
   f ☐ Sum up all the opinions.

🎧 **4** **Listen to the students. Write *Y* (Yusuf), *L* (Lara) or *T* (Thiago).**
4.11   Who ...

   1   suggests ideas (two people)?   ___ ___
   2   interrupts politely?   ___
   3   asks other people for their opinion and sums up the opinions?   ___

Could you be a volunteer with us?

Have you got enough time to help us? All ages are welcome.

Don't give us your money – give us your time!

Together we can make our park better!

Your community needs you!

WHAT?

Help us to make the park a cleaner space for the whole community.

WHERE?

Greenhill Park

WHO?

We have a team of five volunteers, but there's too much work for us. We need more volunteers.

WHEN?

10 am every Saturday. Meet at the park café.

WHY?

It helps your community! There aren't enough people using the park. We want more people to use it.

WHAT ARE THE BENEFITS?

We need only an hour of your time once a week.

You can get fitter and have fun.

It's one of the best ways to make new friends and make a difference!

PLAN

5   **Work in groups. Plan a poster for a volunteer project. Complete the steps below.**

- Choose an idea for a volunteer project. Use the ideas below or your own.
  - Teach older people how to use the latest gadgets.
  - Help at an after-school or local sports club for younger students.
  - Work in an animal shelter.
- Think of phrases to attract volunteers.
- Prepare your poster.
- Add photos.

PRESENT

6   **Display your poster on your classroom wall. Remember to include useful information for volunteers, photos and follow the tips in *How to* agree as a group.**

CHECK

7   **Look at your classmates' posters. Would you like to work on their projects? Vote for the best poster.**

VOCABULARY

1 Complete the conversations with the pairs of verbs in the box.

borrow / owe   pay / lend   spend / save   sell / earn

1 **A** Can you _____ me £2 for a coffee?

   B Don't worry. I can _____ for yours.

2 **A** Those people _____ hats at the market.

   B Yes, but they don't _____ much money.

3 **A** Shall I _____ my money for the future?

   B No! Why don't you _____ it now? Let's go shopping.

4 **A** Could I _____ some money for the bus?

   B Sure, but you now _____ me £5!

2 Read the descriptions and write the correct job.

1 I give my free time to help people. I don't earn any money but I love my job. _____

2 I've got a difficult job in a hospital. I'm not a normal doctor or a nurse. _____

3 I keep our community safe. I can arrest people who are breaking the law. _____

4 I treat very ill people at home and then take them to hospital. _____

LANGUAGE IN ACTION

3 Complete the quiz with the comparative or superlative form of the adjectives. Then decide if the sentences are *T* (true) or *F* (false).

1 Basketball players are usually _____ than footballers. (tall) ____

2 Finland is _____ country in the world. (happy) ____

3 Chris Hemsworth is _____ than Chris Evans. (old) ____

4 The Istanbul Cevahir shopping mall is _____ in the world. (big) ____

5 A hippo is _____ than a lion. (dangerous) ____

6 New York is _____ city to live in. (expensive) ____

4 Put the words in the correct order.

1 lifeguard / you're / too / be / young / to / a

   _____

2 a / money / I / drink / to / haven't / got / enough / buy

   _____

3 room / there / too / people / were / the / many / in

   _____

4 much / night / we / last / spent / too / money

   _____

5 Complete the blog with *too, too many, too much, (not) enough* and the comparative or superlative form of the adjectives. Use *than* if necessary.

All about Holly ♥

Appearance She's [1]_____ (tall) me and she's got [2]_____ (long) hair. So, I'm [3]_____ (short) her in two ways!

Personality She always makes me laugh. She's [4]_____ (funny) and [5]_____ (happy) person I know!

Sport Holly's [6]_____ (good) sport is basketball. Unfortunately, the school team has got [7]_____ players at the moment, so she only plays for fun.

Jobs She wants to be a firefighter. She's [8]_____ (brave) me – that job is [9]_____ (dangerous). There are [10]_____ things to say about Holly – I don't have [11]_____ time now. I've got [12]_____ homework.

Self-assessment

I can use words to talk about money.   ☹ 😐 🙂

I can use words to talk about caring jobs.   ☹ 😐 🙂

I can use *could* and *couldn't*.   ☹ 😐 🙂

I can use comparative and superlative adjectives.   ☹ 😐 🙂

I can use *too, too much, too many* and *(not) enough*.   ☹ 😐 🙂

LEARN TO ... ORGANISE YOUR HOMEWORK
When you organise your homework, you study and use your time better.

1 Do the quiz. Find out your score. Do you agree with what it says about you? Discuss the results with a partner.

Homework superstar?

Knowing what to do
When your teacher gives you homework, do you …
a write it in your notebook or homework diary?
b write it on your hand?
c listen but then forget?

Organising your time
When do you do your homework?
a After school or at the weekend.
b Sometimes after school, sometimes before.
c Always while I'm having breakfast!

Deciding what comes first
You have too much homework and not enough time. Do you …
a do the most important things first?
b do the easiest things first?
c look at your books but never start?

Concentrating
While you're doing your homework, do you …
a switch off your phone?
b try not to look at your phone?
c spend a lot of time checking your phone?

Results
a = 2 points   **b** = 1 points   **c** = 0 point

6-8: You're a superstar! You organise your homework well.
3-5: Not bad! You try to organise your homework, but our advice can help.
0-2: Oh, dear! You really need our advice!

2 Complete Esma's homework diary with the words in the box.

> difficult   first   For when?   Homework   hours   Notes   Other things   Subject

Date	1 _____	2 _____	3 _____	4 _____
Mon 11 Feb	English	Page 27, Exercise 4	Mon 18 Feb	☺ Nice and easy!
Tues 12 Feb	Science	Label the parts of the plant.	Thurs 14 Feb	This is 5_____ – ask Azra for help.
Wed 13 Feb	History Maths	Page 36 Study for the test.	Thurs 14 Feb Fri 15 Feb	Do maths 6_____ – there's a LOT to study!
Thurs 14 Feb	English	Write story.	Tues 19 Feb	I need about two 7_____ .
Fri 15 Feb		No homework!		
8_____ Remember Zoe's party on Saturday afternoon! ☺				

OWN IT!

3 Complete your own homework diary for next week.

5

DREAM HOUSES

LEARNING OUTCOMES
I can ...
- understand texts about different homes and doing household chores
- describe a photograph
- write a description of a house
- understand how to use (not) as + adjective + as, (not) + adjective + enough and have to/don't have to
- talk about furniture and household chores
- make spidergrams to record vocabulary, use techniques to answer multiple-choice questions and use word families.

Start it!

1 Look at the photo. Would you like to live in this house?
2 Before you watch, where do you live?
3 Why did people build homes in mountains? Watch and check.
4 What other unusual homes are there?

Watch video 5.1

Language in action 5.2 p61

Language in action 5.3 p63

Everyday English 5.4 p64

Globetrotters 5.5 p66

VOCABULARY
Furniture

🎧 1 (5.01) Match the words in the box with 1–13 in the pictures. Listen, check and repeat.

armchair	☐	bookcase	☐
carpet	☐	ceiling	1
chest of drawers	☐	cupboard	☐
desk	☐	floor	☐
fridge	☐	picture	☐
shelves	☐	sink	☐
wardrobe	☐		

🎧 2 (5.02) Listen and match the speakers (1–4) with the rooms in the box. There is one extra room.

bathroom	☐	bedroom	☐	kitchen	☐
living room	☐	study	☐		

🎧 3 (5.02) Listen again and circle the words in Exercise 1 that you hear.

🛡 LEARN TO LEARN

Using spidergrams

Recording words in different ways will help you remember them. One way is to create spidergrams.

4 Complete the spidergram using the words in Exercise 1 and your own ideas.

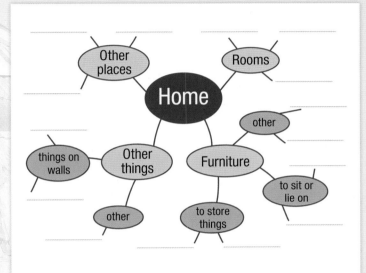

🔊 Use it!

5 Describe the furniture in a room in your home. Your partner listens and draws the room.

> *My bedroom has a wardrobe, a chest of drawers, and two pictures on the wall …*

Explore it! 🖱

Guess the correct answer.

The oldest bookcases in the world are … years old.

a 200 **b** 400 **c** 600

Find an interesting fact about furniture. Then write a question for your partner.

READING
A magazine article

🗨 **1** **Look at the pictures. Discuss the questions.**

1 What's unusual about these homes?

2 Who do you think lives in them?

🎧 **2** **Read the article. Match the pictures with the houses.**
5.03

Amazing
homes

Everyone's home is special, but some homes are really amazing…

Keret House, Poland
A Polish architect designed this house for an Israeli author. ¹**It**'s in a space between two apartment blocks in Warsaw. To enter the house, you climb through a trap door in the floor of the living room. The living room is wide enough for a small sofa, but the back of the house is only as wide as a large armchair! There's a tiny bathroom upstairs, and a tiny kitchen with a sink and a fridge … but you need to stand in another room to open ²**it**!

Nautilus House, Mexico
Nautilus House isn't as tiny as Keret House, but it's also very strange. Its owners – a Mexican couple and their two children – thought ordinary houses weren't close enough to nature. ³**They** wanted their home to feel like a beautiful, colourful shell. Everything in Nautilus House is curved: the floors, the ceilings and, of course, all the furniture.

The PAS House, USA
Lots of kids love skateboarding, but not many kids are as crazy about ⁴**it** as Pierre André Senizergues. Senizergues learned to skateboard at school in France and later became the world champion. He designed the PAS House as a dream home for skateboarders. You can skate in every room. You can even skate on the furniture ⁵**there**, and your mum won't shout at you!

3 **Read the article again and correct the sentences.**

1 The entrance to Keret House is through the kitchen. _The entrance to Keret House is through the living room._

2 Five people live in Nautilus House.

3 The rooms in Nautilus House have straight walls.

4 The PAS House is in France.

5 An architect had the idea for the PAS House.

4 **Look at the underlined words in the text. What do they refer to? Circle the correct answers.**

1 *a Polish architect / Keret House*

2 *the fridge / the sink*

3 *Ordinary houses / The couple*

4 *the PAS house / skateboarding*

5 *the PAS House / France*

5 **Match the words with the definitions.**

1	architect	a	a home for a sea animal
2	author	b	a door in the floor
3	apartment block	c	a writer
4	trap door	d	not straight
5	shell	e	a building with homes in it
6	curved	f	a person who designs buildings

🎙 **Voice it!**

6 **Discuss the questions.**

1 Which house do you like most?

2 Why do you like it?

3 Do you know any other unusual houses? Describe them.

🎲 **Finished? p122 Ex 1**

LANGUAGE IN ACTION

(*not*) *as* + adjective + *as*,
(*not*) + adjective + *enough*

Watch video 5.2
What's wrong with bedroom 1? Why does the vlogger prefer bedroom 3?

The back of the house is only ¹_____ (wide) a large armchair.	The living room is ²_____ (wide) for a small sofa.
Nautilus House is ³_____ (not / tiny) Keret house.	They thought ordinary houses were ⁴_____ (not / close) to nature.

1 **Complete the examples in the table above with *as* or *enough* and the words in brackets. Use the article on page 60 to help you.**

2 **Circle the correct words. Check your answers in the article on page 60.**

   1 Keret House *is as wide as* / (*isn't as wide as*) other houses in Warsaw.

   2 Keret House is *large enough* / *not large enough* for a kitchen.

   3 The Mexican couple think that straight walls are *as interesting as* / *not as interesting as* curved walls.

   ◉ **Get it right!**

   We never put adjectives after *enough*.

   I'm not tall enough. **NOT** ~~I'm not enough tall.~~

3 **Complete the sentences with *as ... as* or *enough* and the adjective in brackets.**

   1 My bedroom isn't ___as big as___ my sister's. (big)

   2 I'm not _____ to reach the top shelf. (tall)

   3 Is this sofa _____ for us all to sit on it? (wide)

   4 That car is _____ an apartment. (expensive)

4 **Complete the second sentence so that it has the same meaning as the first. Use (*not*) *as ... as* or (*not*) *enough* and the adjective in brackets.**

   1 We can't put a sofa in this small room.
      This room _isn't large enough_ for a sofa. (large)

   2 My room is tidier than my sister's room.
      My sister's room _____ my room. (tidy)

   3 A microwave is quicker than a cooker.
      A cooker _____ a microwave. (quick)

   4 Enes is 18 now so he can drive a car.
      Enes _____ to drive a car. (old)

🎧 5.04 5 **Complete the text using (*not*) *as ... as* or (*not*) *enough* and the adjectives in brackets. Then listen and check.**

Kids' toys aren't cheap these days, but not many toys are ¹*as expensive as* (expensive) Astolat Dollhouse Castle. It's an American doll's house – but it isn't an ordinary one. It's ²_____ (tall) a small Christmas tree and ³_____ (heavy) a horse. The castle was the idea of an American artist, Elaine Diehl, and it took her 13 years to build. Of course, it isn't really a toy. It's a work of art, and it's ⁴_____ (perfect) to be in a museum.

The furniture is ⁵_____ (small) to fit in your hand, and it's ⁶_____ (beautiful) the furniture in a real palace. The tiny sofas and beds are ⁷_____ (soft) the real things. The books on the shelves aren't ⁸_____ (large) to read, but they have real pages. One thing that isn't small is the price – over $8 million! Are you ⁹_____ (rich) to buy it?

 Use it!

6 **Write one true sentence and one false sentence about places in the world with (*not*) *as ... as* or (*not*) *enough*.**

   The Amazon is as long as the Nile.

   _____

   _____

7 **Say your sentences to a partner. Can you guess which sentences are true?**

   🏁 **Finished? p122 Ex 2**

VOCABULARY AND LISTENING
Household chores

1 🎧 5.05 Match the phrases in the box with the pictures. Listen, check and repeat.

clean (the kitchen)	☐	do the ironing	1
do the washing	☐	do the washing-up	☐
empty (the washing machine)	☐	load the dishwasher	☐
		make your bed	☐
tidy up (the living room)	☐	vacuum (the carpet)	☐

2 🎧 5.06 Complete the note with verbs in Exercise 1. Then listen and check.

Hi kids, I'm working all day today. Can you please help with some things around the house while I'm out?

<u>Ollie</u>: Please ¹ <u>clean</u> the kitchen and ² _____ the dishwasher with the plates and cups from breakfast. Can you also ³ _____ up the living room, please, and ⁴ _____ the carpet?

<u>Mia</u>: Tidy up your bedroom and ⁵ _____ your bed. Then can you please ⁶ _____ the ironing for me? The clothes are still in the washing machine, so ⁷ _____ that first.

Thanks, kids. I'll see you this evening.

Love, Dad

Use it!

3 How often do you do the chores in Exercise 1? Compare with your partner.

> *I do the washing-up every day!*

Street interviews

4 Look at the diagram. Does the information surprise you?

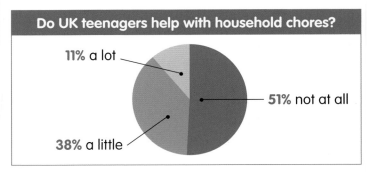

Do UK teenagers help with household chores?

- 11% a lot
- 51% not at all
- 38% a little

🛡 LEARN TO LEARN

Answering multiple-choice questions
Before you listen, read the questions and options carefully. Try to guess the answers before you listen.

5 💬 Read the questions in Exercise 6. Discuss with a partner which answers are probably wrong.

6 🎧 5.07 Listen and circle the correct answers.

1 In the kitchen, Cindy …
 a cooks every day. b loads the dishwasher.
 c does the washing-up.

2 Kim and her sister help with the household chores …
 a every morning. b at the weekend.
 c during school holidays.

3 Kim doesn't like …
 a cleaning the bathroom.
 b vacuuming the living room.
 c practising the piano.

4 When Tim does the ironing, he likes …
 a listening to music. b moving around.
 c doing his homework.

LANGUAGE IN ACTION
have to/don't have to

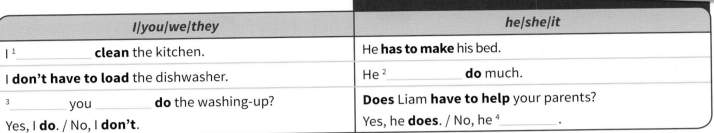

Watch video 5.3
How does Syd from Brazil help in the restaurant? What does Harumi have to clean?

I/you/we/they	he/she/it
I ¹_____ **clean** the kitchen.	He **has to make** his bed.
I **don't have to load** the dishwasher.	He ²_____ **do** much.
³_____ you _____ **do** the washing-up?	**Does** Liam **have to help** your parents?
Yes, I **do**. / No, I **don't**.	Yes, he **does**. / No, he ⁴_____ .

> Pronunciation p141–142

1 Complete the examples in the table above with the correct form of *have to/ don't have to*.

2 Complete the sentences with the correct form of *have to*.

1 Cindy *has to* (+) tidy up the kitchen.
2 Kim and Maisie _____ (+) do a lot of homework.
3 They _____ (–) do housework on school days.
4 Liam _____ (–) help a lot.
5 Tim _____ (+) do the ironing.

3 Circle the correct answer.

1 I … do the gardening this weekend because my parents are on holiday.
   a has to   ⓑ have to
   c doesn't have to

2 … to do a lot of homework at the weekends?
   a Does you have   b Do you have
   c Do you has

3 We … go to school on Monday because it's a national holiday.
   a don't have to
   b doesn't have to
   c have to

4 Dad … do the cooking in the evenings because Mum works then.
   a has to   b have to
   c doesn't have to

4 Complete the sentences with the correct form of *have to* and a verb from the box.

> do   help   go   work

1 The children *don't have to go* to school in summer.
2 Sam_____ with chores because he's only four.
3 I _____ the ironing on Saturdays and it's so boring.
4 _____ your mum _____ at the weekends?

5 Complete the text with the correct form of *have to* and the verbs in brackets. Then listen and check.
(5.10)

¹*Do* you *have to help* (help) with the housework? ²_____ you _____ (tidy) your bedroom or clean the kitchen? 13-year-old Martha Pinter and her 9-year-old brother, Ben, ³_____ (do) more than most young people of their age. They live on a farm in Queensland, Australia, and all the family ⁴_____ (share) the work. Martha ⁵_____ (get up) early to milk the cows. In spring, she also ⁶_____ (look after) the new lambs – that's her favourite job. Ben ⁷_____ (collect) the hens' eggs before breakfast. However, Martha and Ben ⁸_____ (not catch) the bus to school every day. There isn't a school near their farm, so they ⁹_____ (have) all their lessons at home.

Use it!

6 Think of questions to ask your partner using *have to*. Ask and answer your questions.

Does your dad have to do the ironing at the weekend?

No, he doesn't. I have to do it!

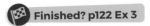

Finished? p122 Ex 3

SPEAKING
Discussing a photo

🎧 **1** Listen to the conversation. Who likes the room
5.11   more, Oscar or Nina?

OSCAR	Hey, Nina. Look at this photo – it's Liam's bedroom in his new house.
NINA	Oh! It looks big enough for two people. Does he have to share it?
OSCAR	No, it's all his. Actually, it isn't as big as it looks. There's a large mirror in the ¹background, so it looks bigger.
NINA	Oh yes, I see. ² _____ thing on the wall?
OSCAR	It's a clock. What do you think of the colour of the walls?
NINA	Hmm. I'm not convinced.
OSCAR	Really? I think it looks awesome! I don't think much of those curtains, though.
NINA:	Me neither. And what's that ³ _____ the bottom? Is it a carpet?
OSCAR	Yes, I think so. I quite like it. And I love those pictures ⁴ _____ the left.
NINA	Me too. They look great.

🎧 **2** Complete the conversation with the phrases
5.11   from the *Useful language* box. Then listen
and check.

> **Useful language**
>
> at the bottom/top   in the background
> on the left/right   What's that … ?

3 Look at the *Everyday English* box. Find and
underline the phrases in the conversation.

> **Watch video 5.4**
> **Everyday English**
>
> I'm not convinced.
> It looks awesome!
> Me neither.   Me too.

4 Match the phrases in the *Everyday English* box
with these phrases.

1 I feel the same way (after a positive statement).
   _____

2 I feel the same way (after a negative statement).
   _____

3 I don't think I like it. _____

4 It looks great. _____

PLAN

5 Write about a room. Make notes about the
photo below or your own photo.

Who does the room belong to? _____
What is in it? _____

SPEAK

6 Practise the conversation with your partner.
Remember to use adjectives with *(not) as …
as* and *(not) enough*, *have to/don't have to*, the
vocabulary from this unit, and phrases from
the *Useful language* and *Everyday English*
boxes.

CHECK

7 Work with another pair. Listen to their
conversation and complete the notes.

Who does the room belong to? _____
What is in it? _____
_____

WRITING
A description of a house

1 Look at the information about the competition and the photo. What can you guess about Olivia's dream house? Discuss with a partner.

2 Read Olivia's description of her dream house. Match headings a–c with paragraphs 1–3.

   a What has the house got?

   b Where is the house?

   c What is the best thing about the house?

3 Read the description again. Draw Olivia's house and garden in your notebook.

4 Find and <u>underline</u> the *Useful language* phrases in the description. Answer the questions.

   1 Which go at the end of a sentence?

   _____ , _____

   2 Which goes before a thing? _____

> **Useful language**
>
> also   as well   as well as   too

Describe your dream house and win a digital camera!

1 ☐ I'd like to tell you about my dream house. It's near the beach on a sunny island. It has to be near the sea because I love swimming.

2 ☐ The house has got big windows and a fantastic view of the sea. There's a lovely garden, too. It's large enough for people to play in and it's also got a swimming pool. As well as a pool, there's a skatepark. Inside the house, there's a huge fish tank. It's full of beautiful tropical fish.

3 ☐ But the really special thing about my house is the technology. There are robots in every room. I think they're as intelligent as humans. They cook the meals and do the washing-up. They make my bed and they tidy the living room as well. I don't have to do any chores.

Olivia Reed (13), Newcastle

Write a description of your own dream house.

PLAN

5 Imagine your dream house and make notes.

   1 Where is your house? _____

       Why do you like it? _____

   2 What rooms, furniture and other things has it got? _____

   3 Why is this your dream house? _____

WRITE

6 Write your description. Remember to include adjectives with *(not) as … as*, *(not) enough* and *have to/don't have to* and phrases from the *Useful language* box.

CHECK

7 Do you …

- have three paragraphs?
- describe what the house has got?
- explain why this is your dream house?

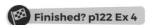 **Finished? p122 Ex 4**

AROUND THE WORLD

Globetrotters
Watch video 5.5
Living in a ger

READING
An encyclopaedia entry

1 Look at the photos. Where are these homes? Who lives there? What do you know about the homes?

🎧 2 Read the encyclopaedia entry. Check your answers to Exercise 1.
5.12

- Do you like moving house? Why?
- What does 'ger' mean in Mongolian?
- Would you like to live in a ger?

3 Read the entry again. Match headings a–e with paragraphs 1–5.

a Why use igloos?
b Keeping warm
c Who are the Inuit?
d Life inside
e How to build an igloo

LIFE IN AN INUIT IGLOO

1 ☐ The Inuit are the native people of the Arctic Circle. Today, they usually live in modern houses in small villages. Until recently, however, they still used their famous houses made of snow – igloos.

2 ☐ The Arctic isn't warm enough to farm, so the Inuit had a nomadic life. This means they travelled during the year to find food. Every winter and summer, the Inuit travelled thousands of kilometres across the frozen Arctic sea. All nomads have to make temporary homes while they travel, and in summer, the Inuit lived in tents made from animal skins, called tupiqs. Igloos were their traditional winter homes.

3 ☐ Snow is a perfect material for building. It's as light as wood and easy to cut. The snow has to be dry and hard enough to make good blocks, because wet snow doesn't have the strength an igloo needs. The Inuit make a dome shape by putting the snow blocks in a spiral. This is quick to build and creates a very strong structure.

4 ☐ The heat inside an igloo comes from people's bodies only, but this is warm enough to keep the igloo comfortable. This is because snow is a good insulator. In other words, it keeps the cold out and the warmth in. The entrance is a tunnel that goes under the walls. The heavy, cold air always stays in the tunnel and the light, warm air stays in the igloo.

5 ☐ Igloos don't have windows, but there are small holes in the walls. These let in clean air and let out dangerous smoke from the small oil lamps. Traditionally, the Inuit didn't have any furniture, but a platform of snow just below the ceiling provided a simple sofa and bed in the warmest part of the igloo. Inuit families spent all winter in small igloos with no furniture, no bathroom … and no Internet.

4 Are the sentences *T* (true) or *F* (false)?

1 The Inuit live in the Arctic Circle. _____

2 In summer, the Inuit are farmers. _____

3 Dry snow isn't as strong as wet snow. _____

4 An igloo doesn't take long to make. _____

5 There are no heaters in an igloo. _____

6 The tunnel lets smoke escape. _____

Word families (2)

Many nouns have a related adjective. We usually form the related adjective or noun by adding extra letters. We sometimes need to change other letters.

Noun	Adjective	Extra letters
beauty	beauti**ful**	-ful
tru**th**	true	-th

5 Complete the table. Use the example to help you.

Noun	Adjective
tradition	¹ *traditional*
² _____	strong
comfort	³ _____
⁴ _____	warm
danger	⁵ _____

6 Complete the sentences with the correct form of the words in brackets. Use the extra letters in the box.

> -ful   -ic   -ous   ~~-ly~~   -th

1 My neighbour isn't very *friendly*. (friend)

2 Andy's bedroom is full of photos of _____ people. (fame)

3 Hassan found a _____ website for his homework. (help)

4 Ava's garden is the _____ of a football pitch! (long)

5 My sister runs a lot. She's really _____. (athlete)

🗨 7 Ask each other to say sentences with words in Exercises 5 and 6.

> *Tell me a sentence with the adjective of fame.*

> *Ed Sheeran is a famous singer.*

Explore it! 🖱

Guess the correct answer.

The Inuit live in Canada, Alaska and …

a Iceland.   b Greenland.   c Norway.

Find three more interesting facts about the Inuit. Choose your favourite fact and write a question for your partner.

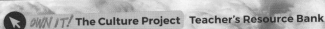 🖱 *OWN IT!* The Culture Project   Teacher's Resource Bank

VOCABULARY

1 Complete the sentences with words for furniture.

1 The _____ on my walls are full of books.

2 This room needs some nice _____ on the walls.

3 Can you put this milk back in the _____, please?

4 I do all my homework on the kitchen table because I haven't got a _____ in my room.

5 We painted the _____ in my bedroom blue. It looks nice when you look up at it.

6 There's a lovely soft _____ on the floor.

2 Complete the 'to do' list from John's mum.

> **John: To do on Saturday morning**
> • Please tidy your bedroom and make your
> ¹ _____ 🖼️ .
> • After breakfast, load the ² _____ 📺 and do the ³ _____ 🔲 in the sink.
> • Empty the ⁴ _____ ⚪ when it finishes, but don't do the ⁵ _____ 🔲 ! I'll do that when I get home.

LANGUAGE IN ACTION

3 Complete Katy's email with *as … as* or *enough* and the adjective in brackets.

> Hi Livvy,
>
> I'm living in a new house. It isn't ¹ _____ (big) our old one, but it's ² _____ (big) for all of us and we like it. We're in the middle of the countryside, but the nearest town is ³ _____ (close) to go shopping or to the cinema. The best thing is the garden. It isn't ⁴ _____ (beautiful) yours, but I like it! Anyway, it's ⁵ _____ (good) for our pet rabbit. He's ⁶ _____ (happy) a baby, running about in the sunshine.
>
> Write soon with your news.
>
> Katy

4 Complete the conversation. Use the words in brackets with *as … as*, *enough* or the correct form of *have to/don't have to*.

RENA	Have you seen Bianca's new house? She told me it isn't ¹ _____ (nice) her old one.
MIKE	Really? The garden's amazing. It's ² _____ (large) a football pitch!
RENA	Wow!
MIKE	Well maybe it's not that big. But it's ³ _____ (big) to play football anyway.
RENA	So why isn't she ⁴ _____ (happy) she was in her old house?
MIKE	Because now she ⁵ _____ (share) her room with her little sister.
RENA	I've got a little sister so I know how she feels! ⁶ _____ she still _____ (take) the bus to school?
MIKE	No, her new house is ⁷ _____ (close) for her to walk. She and her sister are pleased because they ⁸ _____ (wake up) as early as before.

🧍 Self-assessment

I can use words to talk about furniture.	😕	😐	🙂
I can use words to talk about household chores.	😕	😐	🙂
I can use *(not)* as + adjective + *as*.	😕	😐	🙂
I can use *(not)* enough + adjective.	😕	😐	🙂
I can use *have to/don't have to*.	😕	😐	🙂

LEARN TO ... USE A MEMORY JOURNEY

A memory journey connects images with words. It can help you remember lists of vocabulary.

1 Imagine you're going to use a memory journey to learn the words in the box for a test. Put steps a–d in order.

> awesome   beautiful   dangerous
> famous   traditional   warm

a ☐ Imagine walking around your house, looking at those pieces of furniture.

b ☐ Think of an image of each word you need to learn and put it with one of the pieces of furniture. Be creative!

c ☐ Think of six pieces of furniture in your house, for example, the shelves in your bedroom, the living room carpet, the kitchen sink.

d ☐ Think of your house.

2 Match these thoughts with one of the steps a–d in Exercise 1.

> *First I walk through the front door and into the living room. My dad and brother are having an awesome game of football on the carpet. Then I go into the kitchen. I see a famous singer cleaning the sink. After that I go up to my bedroom. There's a dangerous snake on one of the shelves. Next ...*

OWN IT!

5 Use rooms and objects in your school to make a memory journey for the words in the box.

> comfortable   curved   friendly
> helpful   nervous   strong

💬 6 Close your books. Can you remember the words in Exercise 5? Describe your memory journey to your partner.

💬 7 What other places could you use for memory journeys? Discuss with a partner.

3 Follow the steps in Exercise 1 to make your own memory journey for the words in the box.

💬 4 Describe your memory journey in Exercise 3 to your partner. Who has the strangest or funniest images?

6

HIDDEN DANGER

LEARNING OUTCOMES

I can ...

- understand texts about dangers at the beach and in the desert
- make suggestions
- write a blog post
- understand how to use *should/shouldn't*, *must/mustn't*, the zero conditional and first conditional
- talk about accidents and injuries and parts of the body
- use places to remember words and use pictures to predict a story
- work in a group and make an information leaflet.

▶ Start it!

1   Look at the photo. What dangerous thing can you see?
2   Before you watch, when do you not have your phone with you?
3   Where are there special smartphone-pavements? Watch and check.
4   Do you use your phone while walking in the street?

Watch video 6.1

Language in action 6.2 p73

Language in action 6.3 p75

Everyday English 6.4 p76

VOCABULARY
Accidents and injuries

🎧 6.01 **1** Complete the phrases with the words in the box. Listen, check and repeat.

be bitten	be stung	break	bruise	burn	~~cut~~
fall off	hit	scratch	slip	sprain	trip over

cut your finger

_____ by a bee

_____ your head

_____ your arm

_____ a chair

_____ your ankle

_____ by a mosquito

_____ your hand

_____ your leg

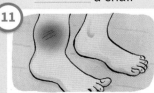
_____ your horse

_____ your leg

Get it right!

We usually use words like *my*, *your*, *his*, *her* when we talk about parts of the body.

*I hit **my** head. Did Lisa burn **her** hand?*

🎧 6.02 **2** Listen. Write the accidents and injuries in Exercise 1 that you hear.

1 _____   4 _____

2 _____   5 _____

3 _____

🛡 LEARN TO LEARN

Using places to remember words
It can help you to remember new words if you think of where they might happen.

3 Think of a place where each accident in Exercise 1 might happen.

trip over a chair – in the classroom
_____

💬 **4** Test your partner. Say a place that you thought of in Exercise 3. Your partner guesses the accident or injury you thought of.

The kitchen.   *Cut your finger?*

Use it!

5 Ask and answer these questions about the phrases in Exercise 1.

1 When was the last time one of these things happened to you or someone you know?

2 Where did it happen?

3 What happened?

Explore it! 🖱

Is the sentence *T* (true) or *F* (false)?

All bees can sting. ☐

Find an interesting fact about another animal that bites or stings. Then write a question for your partner to answer.

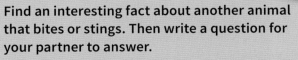

READING
An online article

1 **Check the meaning of the words in the box. Can you see them in the photos?**

> animals that sting   broken glass   large waves
> quicksand   rip currents   shark attack

🎧 2 **Read the article. Which danger in Exercise 1 isn't in the article?**
6.03

3 **Find words in the article that mean:**
1 difficult to find _____
2 quickly _____
3 something dangerous from an animal _____
4 move your body to get free _____
5 when the sea goes in and out at different times of the day _____

4 **Are the sentences T (true) or F (false)?**
1 Some beaches are more dangerous than others. T
2 Rip currents move away from the beach. ____
3 Crocodiles don't live near the sea. ____
4 The blue-ringed octopus is big and ugly. ____
5 One blue-ringed octopus can kill a lot of people. ____
6 All British beaches are safe. ____

🔊 **Voice it!**

5 **Discuss the questions.**
1 What other dangers at the beach can you think of?
2 What other dangerous places do some people like to visit? Why do they go there?

🏁 **Finished? p123 Ex 1**

DANGERS AT THE BEACH

Beaches promise sun, sand and fun and are usually safe places to go, but accidents can happen. You can slip and break your leg, or step on some glass and cut your foot. Ouch! Some beaches around the world have hidden dangers, however, and you should take extra care.

HAWAII

It's great for surfing, but beaches in Hawaii also have dangerous rip currents. Rip currents happen when water moves swiftly away from the beach. They are difficult to see and can move very fast. They can take people far out to sea, so swimmers mustn't try to swim against them. Instead, they should swim sideways along the beach until they get to safer waters.

AUSTRALIA

Everyone knows that huge sharks sometimes swim near Australian beaches, and crocodiles can also come very near. You must always be careful. Never swim when there isn't a lifeguard on the beach.

Sharks and crocodiles aren't the only danger on Australia's beaches. The beautiful Australian blue-ringed octopus, for example, is as small as your hand. But you mustn't go near them. They have enough venom to kill ten people!

UK

The sand can be as unsafe as the sea, and on some British beaches it can kill! Dangerous quicksand is full of water and it's very easy for people to sink in it. You shouldn't kick or struggle. You must move very slowly and carefully to get out … before the tide comes in!

WARNING
Dangerous sand

LANGUAGE IN ACTION
should/shouldn't and must/mustn't

Watch video 6.2
What should you do if you get burned?
What should you do with a sprained ankle?

should for advice	*must* for strong advice or a rule
You ¹ _should_ **take** extra care.	You ² _____ always **be** careful.
You ³ _____ **kick** or struggle.	Swimmers ⁴ _____ **try** to swim against them.

> Pronunciation p142

1 Complete the examples in the table above with *should/shouldn't* or *must/mustn't*. Use the article on page 72 to help you.

2 Correct the sentences about the article on page 72.

1 You shouldn't wear sandals on the beach.
   You should wear sandals on the beach.

2 In a rip current, you must swim towards the beach.
   _____

3 You should swim near the blue-ringed octopus.
   _____

4 In quicksand, you should kick and jump.
   _____

3 Circle the correct words.

1 You *should* / (*shouldn't*) swim here. The water isn't clean.

2 You *must* / *mustn't* speak in exams.

3 I think everyone *should* / *must* do a sport. Exercise is good for you.

4 You *must* / *should* wear a seatbelt in the car. It's the law.

5 I think you *should* / *must* learn to speak another language.

6 You *shouldn't* / *mustn't* go outside in shorts. It's cold today.

4 Complete the notice with *should*, *shouldn't*, *must* or *mustn't*. Then listen and check.
6.07

Hi everyone,
Now the spring term is here, I think you
¹ _should_ all think about walking or cycling to school if you can.
Cycling is fun and healthy, but you ² _____ be careful. For example, you ³ _____ ride when the weather is bad, and you ⁴ _____ wear a helmet. That's extremely important. However, you also ⁵ _____ forget that there are rules on the road for cyclists, and you ⁶ _____ learn these rules. The school website has some good advice, such as which clothes you ⁷ _____ wear to cycle, and I think all cyclists ⁸ _____ read it carefully.
One more thing: we need to know which students are cycling to school, so you ⁹ _____ tell Mrs Jones if you plan to cycle. That's a school rule, so you ¹⁰ _____ forget!

🔵 **Use it!**

5 Write rules and advice for staying safe while doing these activities.

ice skating	mountain biking	rock climbing	surfing

_____

_____

6 Read your rules and advice to your partner but don't say the activities. Can they guess them?

You should wear a wetsuit to do this. But you mustn't do it in bad weather. What is it?

Surfing?

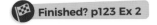 **Finished? p123 Ex 2**

VOCABULARY AND LISTENING
Parts of the body

🎧 **1** Match the words in the box with 1–12 in the
6.08 photo. Listen, check and repeat.

cheek ☐	chest ☐	chin ☐
elbow ☐	forehead ☐1	heel ☐
knee ☐	neck ☐	shoulder ☐
teeth ☐	toe ☐	wrist ☐

2 Complete the sentences with words in Exercise 1.

1 Your _wrist_ is between your hand and your arm.
2 People have ten fingers and ten _____ .
3 Children have 20 _____ and adults have 32.
4 Your _____ is just above your eyes.
5 Your _____ is in the middle of your leg.
6 Your _____ is at the top of your arm.

 Use it!

3 Point to a part of the body in Exercise 1. Name
the part your partner points to.

A radio interview

🛡 **LEARN TO LEARN**

Using pictures to predict a story
Before you listen, look carefully at any pictures and use
them to imagine a story.

4 Look at the pictures in Exercise 6. Choose one
picture from each set of three and use them to
make a story.

🎧 **5** Listen to the interview. What parts of your story
6.09 were correct?

🎧 **6** Listen again. Choose the correct options.
6.09

1 What job does Pam do?

2 What was Jamie doing before his accident?

3 What did Jamie do?

4 What injuries did Jamie get?

💬 **7** Work with your partner to tell Jamie's story. Use
the pictures to help you.

LANGUAGE IN ACTION
Zero conditional and first conditional

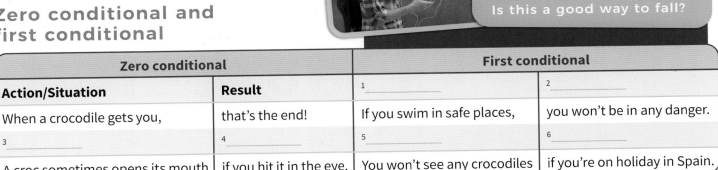

Watch video 6.3
How can you fall off a skateboard safely?
Is this a good way to fall?

Zero conditional		First conditional	
Action/Situation	**Result**	¹ _____	² _____
When a crocodile gets you,	that's the end!	If you swim in safe places,	you won't be in any danger.
³ _____	⁴ _____	⁵ _____	⁶ _____
A croc sometimes opens its mouth	if you hit it in the eye.	You won't see any crocodiles	if you're on holiday in Spain.

1 Complete the headings in the table above with *Action/Situation* or *Result*.

2 Match 1–5 with a–e. Then complete the result with the correct form of the verb in brackets.

1 Accidents happen (happen) _e_
2 If you see a crocodile, ___
3 If a crocodile bites you, ___
4 When a crocodile wants to cool down, ___
5 If a crocodile loses a tooth, ___

a it _____ (try) to pull you under the water.
b another one _____ (grow).
c it _____ probably _____ (ignore) you.
d it _____ (open) its mouth.
e when you aren't careful.

🎧 6.10 **3** Complete the email with the correct form of the verbs in brackets. Then listen and check.

So you're going to visit Queensland. Great idea! If you
¹ like (like) beaches and forests, you ² _____ (love)
Port Douglas. It's amazing. It usually ³ _____ (take)
about an hour to get there if you ⁴ _____ (get) a bus
from the airport. Buses are quite frequent, so if you
⁵ _____ (miss) one, you ⁶ _____ (not have) a long
wait. Of course, if you ⁷ _____ (not mind) spending
more money, there ⁸ _____ (be) always taxis at the
airport, too! If you ⁹ _____ (visit) Four Mile Beach,
you ¹⁰ _____ (have) a great time surfing. But be
careful! If you ¹¹ _____ (not see) anyone else in the
water, it probably ¹² _____ (mean) there are sharks
or jellyfish in the sea!
Have fun and take care!

4 Complete the information about the Amazon jungle. Use the words in the box.

go   have   hide   run away

Snakes
Snakes ¹ _____ if they hear people coming. Most snake venom isn't fatal if you ² _____ straight to hospital.

Bigger animals
You probably won't see any jaguars because they ³ _____ when they feel threatened. However, if a jaguar ⁴ _____ young cubs, it is more dangerous.

5 Imagine you're planning a jungle holiday. Write what you will do if the following things happen.

1 If I see a snake on the path, I'll wait for it to go away.
2 If I'm very hot and I find a river, _____
_____.
3 If I'm bitten by a spider, _____
_____.
4 If I get lost, _____.

💬 **Use it!**

6 Say the second half of your sentences in Exercise 5. Can your partner guess the first half?

I'll look for a river to follow.   *If I get lost?*

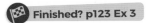 **Finished? p123 Ex 3**

SPEAKING
Making suggestions

🎧 **1** Listen to the conversation. Who knows more
6.11 about mountain bikes, Dan or Hayley?

DAN	Awesome mountain bike, Hayley.
HAYLEY	Thanks, Dan.
DAN	I'd like to get one, too. Do you think I should buy one online?
HAYLEY	Not really. Some online shops aren't very reliable. Their bikes aren't very safe. Anyway, ¹*make sure you don't* buy one without trying it first. ² _____ try The Bike Shack in town? They're really good.
DAN	OK. I'll give them a go.
HAYLEY	And ³ _____ buy a good helmet, too. You can really hurt yourself if you fall off, so you mustn't ride without one.
DAN	Good idea. I think I should find some buddies to ride with, too. What do you think?
HAYLEY	Sure. ⁴ _____ joining my bike club? We go out every weekend.
DAN	Yeah! Nice one, Hayley. I'll do that.

🎧 **2** Complete the conversation with the phrases
6.11 from the *Useful language* box. Then listen and check.

Useful language

How about + *-ing* … ?	Make sure you don't …
Why don't you … ?	You should definitely …

3 Look at the *Everyday English* box. Find and
underline the phrases in the conversation.

Watch video 6.4
Everyday English

Awesome	buddies
I'll give it/them a go.	Nice one

4 Complete the sentences with the *Everyday English*
phrases.

1 _____ snowboard, Maya!

2 Ava said that *Hunts* is a good shop for camping gear. _____

3 You remembered your camera! _____, Beth!

4 That's Alfie. He's one of my surfing _____.

PLAN
5 Think of advice for someone who wants to try a
new sport. Make notes.

What you should or must do: _____

_____

What you shouldn't or mustn't do: _____

_____

SPEAK
6 Practise the conversation with your partner. Ask
for and give advice about the sport. Remember
to use *should/shouldn't* and *must/mustn't*, the
vocabulary from this unit, and phrases from the
Useful language and *Everyday English* boxes.

CHECK
7 Work with another pair. Listen to their
conversation and complete the notes.

What you should or must do: _____

_____

What you shouldn't or mustn't do: _____

_____

What is the best suggestion: _____

_____

WRITING
A blog post

1 Look at the photo. What do you think the blog post is about? Read it and check.

MATT'S BLOG

Thanks for all your comments on my posts. Here are my answers to your questions.

1 ☐
There are cheap boards, but it's best to avoid them. If you want a good board, you need to spend more. I'd say at least £50. Also, make sure you get the right size deck. If you have small feet, you'll need a narrow deck. If it's too wide, you won't be able to control the board.

2 ☐
Yes! When you're a beginner, accidents happen. That's why you need a helmet. It must be a proper skateboarder's helmet, and it must be the right size. If it moves when you shake your head, it's too big.

3 ☐
If you ask me, the street is too dangerous. A skatepark is the best place, but if there isn't one near you, any park will be good.

That's all for now. Have fun, but stay safe!

2 Match questions a–c with paragraphs 1–3.

a Can I skate in the street?

b What board should I buy?

c Should I wear a helmet?

3 Read the blog post again. Which of these opinions does Matt have?

1 Cheap skateboards aren't very good. ☑

2 You can't get a good skateboard for less than £50. ☐

3 For some people, narrow skateboards are best. ☐

4 Your helmet shouldn't move when you wear it. ☐

5 The only safe place for skateboarding is a skatepark. ☐

4 Complete the phrases in the *Useful language* box with words that Matt uses for giving advice.

> **Useful language**
>
> ¹ _____ say   ² _____ sure
>
> ³ _____ why   If you ⁴ _____ me

5 Complete the sentences with the *Useful language* phrases.

1 If you fall off a board, you can really hurt your head. _____ skateboarders wear helmets.

2 If _____ , all skateboarders should wear knee and elbow pads as well.

3 _____ you keep your board in good condition.

4 Many people skate on their own, but _____ it's more fun, and safer, to skate with friends.

Write a blog post to give safety advice.

PLAN

6 Choose an activity. Think of three questions about doing it safely. Make notes for the answers.

1 _____

2 _____

3 _____

WRITE

7 Write your blog post. Remember to include an introduction, three questions and answers, an ending and phrases from the *Useful language* box.

CHECK

8 Do you ...

• answer each question?

• use *should/shouldn't* and *must/mustn't*?

• use vocabulary from this unit?

🏁 **Finished? p123 Ex 4**

THE SCIENCE PROJECT

An information leaflet

1 **Look at the information leaflet. What is it about?**

  a The dangers of the desert

  b How animals live in the desert

2 **Read the leaflet again. Are the sentences _T_ (true) or _F_ (false)?**

  1 All deserts are hot and dry. _F_

  2 Birds can help you in the desert. ____

  3 If you drink water, you won't get heat cramps. ____

  4 A haboob is a desert animal. ____

  5 You shouldn't wear sandals in the desert. ____

  6 Scorpions live in dark places. ____

3 **Complete the table. Put the five dangers in the desert in the correct group.**

Our bodies in the desert	Desert weather	Desert animals
thirst		

How to work in groups

4 **Listen and decide which student worked in these ways. Write _J_ (John), _I_ (Isla) or _P_ (Poppy).**

6.12

  a The group decided what the different jobs were for the project. Each person did a different job. ____

  b The group shared the writing on the project. Each person wrote a different section. ____

  c Each person worked alone first. Then they chose different sections of each person's work to make their poster. ____

5 **Which of the ways of working do you think is best? Why? Share your ideas with a partner.**

Desert survival

Fact file

- A desert is a place with less than 250 mm of rain per year.
- Around 30% of the land on the Earth is desert.
- Only 20% of deserts are sandy. Some have snow.
- Highest temperature in a desert: 56.7 °C (Death Valley, USA)
- Lowest temperature in a desert: -89.2 °C (Antarctica)

Deserts are extremely big, extremely dry and extremely dangerous! If you are lost in one, here are some of the dangers you should know about.

Thirst

What's the danger?

You can't live without water for more than three days.

What should you do?

Walk slowly and rest often. If you don't, you'll lose a lot of water as sweat.

Drink a little and often.

If you see birds, follow them. They'll take you to the nearest water.

Heat cramps

What's the danger?

As well as water, your body needs salt. When you sweat, you lose a lot of salt. If you lose too much, your legs and arms will begin to hurt. This is called heat cramp and in the desert it can be dangerous.

What should you do?

Make sure you carry salt tablets with you. They can save your life!

Sandstorms

What's the danger?

When it gets windy in the desert, sandstorms happen. In Arabic, these huge walls of sand are called *haboob*. They are sometimes more than a kilometre high and can move at 40 kilometres per hour.

What should you do?

If a haboob is coming, you must hide. Sandstorms usually last for a few minutes, but sometimes they last three hours!

Snakes

What's the danger?

If you're in the Arizona Desert and you hear a rattle, it's probably a rattlesnake, and its bite can kill.

What should you do?

Wear strong boots, not sandals. If you see a snake, move away quickly. If it bites you, you must find a doctor as soon as you can.

Scorpions

What's the danger?

There are 2,000 different types of scorpions and 30 of them can kill.

What should you do?

Scorpions live under rocks, so you should be careful where you put your hands!

PLAN

6 **Work in groups. Choose a remote place. Then complete the steps below.**

- Decide how your group will work together.
- Decide on the sections your information leaflet will include.
- Decide what images and diagrams you could include.
- Make a first draft of your leaflet.
- Share your first draft with another group to get their feedback.

PRESENT

7 **Display your information leaflet on your classroom wall. Remember to include different sections, interesting facts and pictures, and the tips in *How to* work in groups.**

CHECK

8 **Ask different groups how they worked. Did they work in the same way as you? Who worked in a group best?**

VOCABULARY

1 Circle the correct words.

1 Sue touched a hot pan and *burned / sprained* her fingers.

2 Juan *slipped / scratched* on some ice.

3 Jane *bruised / fell off* her bike.

4 Andy *was bitten / was stung* by a bee.

5 Masha *fell off / tripped over* a plant in the garden.

6 I *cut / broke* my finger with a knife.

2 Match the words in the box with the descriptions. You can use the words more than once.

> cheek   chin   elbow
> forehead   heel   knee
> shoulder   toe   wrist

1 We have two of these. _____

2 These are parts of your arm. _____

3 These are parts of your leg. _____

4 These are parts of your face. _____

LANGUAGE IN ACTION

3 Complete the sentences with *must/mustn't* or *should/shouldn't* and the verbs in the box.

> sleep   stay   talk   wear

1 You _____ a seatbelt in the car.

2 You _____ in the sun too long.

3 You _____ for eight hours at night.

4 You _____ on your phone while you're riding a bike.

4 Complete the sentences with the zero or first conditional.

1 If you _____ (not take) more care, you _____ (have) an accident.

2 When Gina _____ (go) skateboarding, she always _____ (wear) a helmet.

3 If someone _____ (break) a leg, it _____ (hurt) a lot.

4 If the weather _____ (get) worse, the climbers _____ (be) stuck on the mountain.

5 Snakes _____ usually _____ (not bite) you if you _____ (not disturb) them.

5 Circle the best words to complete the notes.

Stay safe in the forest

Before you go, you ¹*should / shouldn't* tell someone where you're going. If you get lost, it ²*is / will be* easier to find you.

You ³*must / mustn't* take a map. If you ⁴*don't / won't* follow a map, you'll probably get lost.

You ⁵*shouldn't / mustn't* eat mushrooms. Some are very dangerous. If you ⁶*eat / will eat* them, you can get extremely ill.

You ⁷*should / shouldn't* run away from a bear. If you stay calm and walk away slowly, you ⁸*will be / are* OK.

👤 Self-assessment

I can use words to talk about accidents and injuries.	😟 😐 🙂
I can use words to talk about parts of the body.	😟 😐 🙂
I can use *should/shouldn't* and *must/mustn't*.	😟 😐 🙂
I can use the zero conditional and first conditional.	😟 😐 🙂

LEARN TO ... GIVE USEFUL OPINIONS ABOUT YOUR PARTNER'S ENGLISH

Be polite when you give opinions about your partner's English. You can help each other improve.

1 Read the advice about how to give useful opinions. Complete the advice with *should* or *shouldn't*.

> What you ¹_____ do to help your partner improve their English.

> You ²_____ ...
> a say what you think in a horrible way.
> b talk about your partner's personality.
> c say that something is better or worse than it is.
>
> You ³_____ always ...
> d say what you think, but also be nice.
> e say positive things.
> f give ideas for how your partner can improve.

3 Invent a story about an accident. Use one word or phrase from each box and think about the answers to the questions below.

> crocodile   knife   mirror   scissors   snake

> be bitten   break   cut   hit   slip

- What were you doing when the accident happened?
- What happened?
- How did you feel?
- Did anybody help you?
- What happened then?
- What should people do to avoid a similar accident?

2 Match 1–6 with a–f in Exercise 1.

1. ☐ *Well done! You're a really interesting person.*

2. ☐ *That wasn't your best English, but I know you can do better.*

3. ☐ *That was the worst presentation ever!*

4. ☐ *You made some mistakes with the first conditional. Why don't you study the grammar from the unit again?*

5. ☐ *You used lots of adjectives to describe things. That was really nice!*

6. ☐ *Your English was awful!*

4 Take turns to tell your stories. While your partner is speaking, think about what they do well and how they can improve.

OWN IT!

5 Give three helpful opinions about your partner's English. Use the phrases in the box.

> I liked the way you ...
> Why don't you ... ?
> You made some mistakes with ...
> You used ... That was nice!

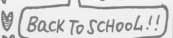

7 GET CONNECTED

LEARNING OUTCOMES

I can ...
- understand texts about technology
- give instructions to explain how to use something
- write an article
- understand how to use the present perfect affirmative and negative, *will/won't*, *may* and *might*, and the infinitive of purpose
- talk about and describe technology and transport
- use collocations, recognise opinions and use words that describe sounds.

▶ Start it!

1 Look at the photo. What type of car is it?
2 Before you watch, what technology have you used today?
3 Who planned the first programmable computer? Watch and check.
4 Which technology would be most difficult to live without?

Watch video 7.1

Language in action 7.2

p85

Language in action 7.3

p87

Everyday English 7.4

p88

Globetrotters 7.5

p90

VOCABULARY
Communication and technology

1 Match the words in the box with 1–11 in the picture. Listen, check and repeat.
7.01

app ☐	chip ☐	device ☐
download ☐	emoji ☐	message ☐
screen ☐	social media ☐	software ☐
upload ☐1	video chat ☐	

2 Complete the sentences with words in Exercise 1. Then listen and check.
7.02

1 My phone fell out of my pocket this morning and the *screen* broke.

2 I can't do a _____ with you right now. I haven't got a camera on my laptop.

3 Most of my friends _____ photos to _____ sites like Instagram.

4 Look at this _____ – it's great for practising new English words. Why don't you _____ it too?

> Pronunciation p142

🛡 LEARN TO LEARN

Collocations
Some words are often used together – we call these collocations. Learn them as phrases.

3 Complete these collocations with words in Exercise 1. There is sometimes more than one possible answer.

1 _____ software
2 use a messaging _____
3 electronic _____
4 send a _____
5 computer _____
6 _____ photos

4 Take turns to start and finish the collocations you made in Exercise 3.

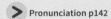

Send a ...   *Send a message?*

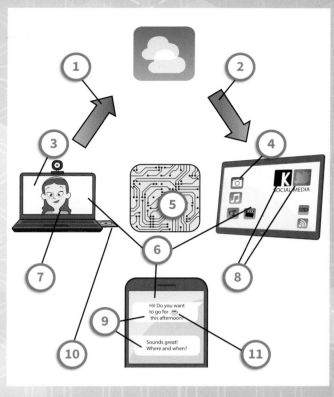

🗣 Use it!

5 Write three sentences about you or people you know using the words in Exercise 1.

My brother has got a lot of apps on his phone.

1 _____
2 _____
3 _____

6 Compare your sentences.

I spend about three hours a day in front of a screen.

I only spend about two hours.

Explore it! 🖱

Is the sentence *T* (true) or *F* (false)?

People with nomophobia feel scared when they don't have their phone with them. ☐

Find an interesting fact about technology. Then write a question for your partner to answer.

READING
A magazine article

1 Look at the photos. What do you think the article is about?

🎧 2 Read the article. Check your answer to Exercise 1.
7.06

○○○
Smartphones and us

Noah Smith investigates how smartphones have changed our lives.

In 1994, the IBM Simon arrived. It was a small computer that made calls! OK, it weighed half a kilo and it didn't have a camera, but it was technically a smartphone. Today's devices are smaller, faster and more fun. Nearly 3 billion people own one, and they have transformed our lives.

○○○ Communication
Smartphone technology has given us many ways to communicate, but the most popular is messaging. Users of one very well-known app, for example, send 60 billion messages every day!

And then there's video. Once, video calls were science fiction – they still are for my grandparents – but for my generation, video chats have become completely normal.

○○○ Entertainment
Gaming apps let us play our favourite games anywhere, anytime on our phones – and that's usually the real reason why my sister hasn't done her homework! She isn't alone. About 34 million people in the UK play online games, and globally the industry is worth billions of dollars. Personally, I'd rather listen to my favourite bands. Smartphones are great for that, too!

○○○ Sharing
Smartphones haven't made us nicer people, but together with social media, they've made it easier for us to have hundreds of 'friends'. 2.5 billion of us have created social media profiles. We post status updates, upload our photos and share videos. Many of us have shared our whole lives online. Which reminds me – I haven't updated my status today!

3 Read the article again. Complete the sentences.

1 Smartphones first appeared in *1994* .
2 The first smartphone weighed _____ kg.
3 _____ people in the world have a smartphone.
4 Users of one well-known messaging app send _____ messages every day.
5 In the UK, about _____ people play games on their mobile devices.
6 _____ people around the world have got social media profiles.

4 Answer the questions.

1 What couldn't computers do before 1994?
   They couldn't make phone calls.
2 Does Noah think the IBM Simon was a very good device? _____
3 Do Noah's grandparents have video chats?
   _____
4 What does Noah's sister enjoy doing?
   _____
5 Does Noah often play games on his phone?
   _____

🎧 5 Complete the words for the numbers. Then listen and check.
7.07

1 1,000,000,000,000 = one _trillion_
2 1,000,000,000 = one _____
3 1,000,000 = one _____
4 1,000 = one _____
5 100 = one _____

🔊 Voice it!

6 Do you agree with the statements below? Discuss with your partner, using the expressions in the box.

> I strongly agree.   I agree.   I'm not sure.
> I disagree.   I strongly disagree.

1 People use their smartphones too much.
2 Children under ten shouldn't have a smartphone.
3 There should be no smartphones in schools.
4 I couldn't live without a smartphone.

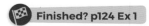 **Finished? p124 Ex 1**

LANGUAGE IN ACTION
Present perfect: affirmative and negative

Watch video 7.2
Name two things Sophia has learned?
What's the best thing that the vlog has given her?

I/you/we/they		he/she/it	
Smartphones [1]_____ **transformed** our lives.		Smartphone technology [2]_____ **given** us many ways to communicate.	
Smartphones [3]_____ **made** us nicer people.		My sister [4]_____ **done** her homework.	

1 Complete the examples in the table above with the correct form of *have (not)*. Use the article on page 84 to help you.

2 Complete the sentences with the present perfect form of the verbs in brackets.
   1 Smartphones <u>have changed</u> our lives. (change)
   2 They _____ easier to carry. (become)
   3 Smartphone technology _____ more interesting. (become)
   4 Smartphones _____ us to communicate. (help)
   5 Noah _____ his online status. (not update)

🎧 3 Complete the conversation with the present perfect form of the verbs. Then listen and check.
7.08

> ask   find   leave   look   ~~lose~~
> not charge   not hear   not see   put

JACK What's wrong, Kim?

KIM I [1]<u>'ve lost</u> my phone. Do you know where it is?

JACK No, I don't. I [2]_____ it ring, either. Perhaps it's in your coat pocket?

KIM I [3]_____ in all my pockets. It's not there.

JACK Perhaps you [4]_____ it in Mum's car.

KIM No, I don't think so. I used it this afternoon, but I can't remember where I left it.

JACK Maybe Mum [5]_____ it somewhere.

KIM No, I [6]_____ her and she says she [7]_____ it. Jack, can you call me?

JACK I think so. I [8]_____ my phone, but I think it's got enough power left. Hang on … OK, I'm calling you …

KIM Here, look! I [9]_____ it. It was in my bag all the time.

4 Answer the questions with present perfect sentences. Use the words in the boxes.

> break   buy   forget

> password   screen   tablet

1 Why can't Orla use her laptop?
   _____

2 Why are Elena and Ruby so happy?
   _____

3 Why is Andrey upset?
   _____

 Use it!

5 Write three sentences about what you have or haven't done today. Use the ideas in the box.

> chat / on social media   check / my emails
> upload / a photo   watch / TV

<u>I've watched breakfast TV.</u>
1 _____
2 _____
3 _____

6 Tell your partner about the things you've done.

> *I haven't uploaded a photo, but I've played my favourite computer game.*

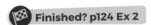 **Finished? p124 Ex 2**

VOCABULARY AND LISTENING
Getting around

🎧 **1** Complete the expressions with the verbs in the box. Listen, check and repeat.
7.09

> catch/get/take   get into   get off   get on
> get out of   go by   ~~go on~~

go on
foot   a train   tram

a plane   a car   a taxi   a bus

2 Complete the sentences with the verbs in Exercise 1. Sometimes there is more than one possible answer.

1 I'm *getting off* this bus at the next stop.
2 My parents have _____ a taxi to the airport because the bus takes too long.
3 I'm late. I want to _____ the train to Ely.
4 I missed the tram so I _____ to work _____ foot.
5 We _____ to the island _____ ferry.

3 Tell your partner about two different ways to get to these places from your home.

> your school   a town in your country   New York

> *To get to school, I can go on foot to the bus stop and then catch a bus. Or I can go by bike.*

A radio interview

💬 **4** Look at the forms of transport in Exercise 5. Will we use them in the future? Discuss with a partner.

🎧 **5** Listen to the radio interview. In which order do they discuss the transport in the pictures?
7.10

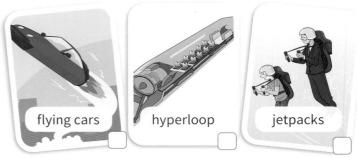

flying cars   hyperloop   jetpacks

🛡 LEARN TO LEARN

Recognising opinions
It's important to understand the difference between facts and opinions. When people give an opinion, they often begin with phrases like these:

in my view …   in my opinion …   I (don't) think …

🎧 **6** Listen again. Which of these opinions does the professor have?
7.10

1 Flying cars aren't the answer to traffic jams. ✓
2 There will be a lot of flying cars soon. ☐
3 People won't use jetpacks to get to work. ☐
4 The hyperloop is just science fiction. ☐
5 The hyperloop will change our lives. ☐

LANGUAGE IN ACTION
will/won't, may and *might*

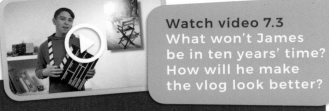

Watch video 7.3
What won't James be in ten years' time? How will he make the vlog look better?

[1]Certain / Uncertain predictions	[2]Certain / Uncertain predictions
It **will** really **change** our lives.	We **may have** jetpacks one day just for fun. We **might see** hyperloops between big cities.
We **won't see** a lot of flying cars in the sky.	They **may not be** useful for getting to work. We **might not need** to wait much longer.

1 Circle the correct words in the headings in the table above.

2 Are these predictions *C* (certain) or *U* (uncertain)?
  1 Cars might be less noisy. U
  2 Every family will have a flying car. ___
  3 In fifty years from now, children may go to school by jetpack. ___
  4 Jetpacks won't be very useful for most people. ___
  5 Everyone will travel by hyperloop. ___
  6 Some people might not want to travel on a hyperloop. ___

3 Listen to Danielle talking about transport in the future. Which of the predictions in Exercise 2 does she make?
7.11

___ , ___ , ___ ,

Use it!

4 Complete the sentences about the future with *will/won't* or *may/might* (*not*). Then compare your opinions in pairs.
  1 People ___ have their own aeroplanes.
  2 People ___ go to work by bike.
  3 We ___ need smartphones.
  4 We ___ use paper.
  5 There ___ be books and magazines.

Infinitive of purpose

to + infinitive
A lot of us catch a bus [1]_____ (go) to work. [2]_____ (solve) the problem, we should invent flying cars. It takes a lot of energy [3]_____ (lift) a person off the ground.

5 Complete the examples in the table above with the correct form of the words in brackets.

6 Match 1–5 with a–e.
  1 Can I borrow your phone
  2 Is there a printer
  3 You can use my laptop
  4 Shall we stop
  5 To get there sooner,

  a to have lunch?
  b to check your email.
  c to make a call?
  d we decided to fly.
  e to print these photos?

Use it!

7 Complete the sentences with your own ideas and tell your partner.
  1 I went to _____ to _____
     _____ .
  2 I bought a _____ to _____
     _____ .
  3 I stopped at/in _____ to _____
     _____ .

I went to London to visit my cousin last summer.

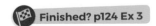 **Finished? p124 Ex 3**

SPEAKING
Giving instructions

1 Listen to the conversation. What is Tom explaining to his dad?
(7.12)

   a How to take a photo

   b How to record a video

TOM   DAD

TOM	So, Dad, before ¹*you start* , switch the camera to record mode. Have you done that?
DAD	Like this?
TOM	Yes, that's right. It needs to be on record mode to film a video. Now, look at this little screen.
DAD	I can't see anything.
TOM	Ah. Remember ² _____ that your hand isn't in front of the camera!
DAD	Is this better?
TOM	Not quite. Look, you need to keep your fingers here. That's it. Now, do you see this button?
DAD	This one?
TOM	No, not that one. This one here. It's ³_____ that it's turned on if you want to record sound. Oh, and ⁴_____ sure that the light is red. That means you're recording. Got that?
DAD	Yes, I think so. Thanks, Tom!

2 Complete the conversation with the phrases from the *Useful language* box. Then listen and check.
(7.12)

> **Useful language**
>
> Before you start, …
>
> It's really important that …
>
> Make sure that …
>
> Remember to check that …

3 Look at the *Everyday English* box. Find and <u>underline</u> the phrases in the conversation.

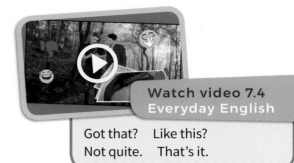

**Watch video 7.4
Everyday English**

> Got that?   Like this?
>
> Not quite.   That's it.

4 Match the phrases in the *Everyday English* box with their meanings.

  1 That's right. _____

  2 Do you understand? _____

  3 This way? _____

  4 Not exactly. _____

PLAN

5 Give instructions for using a type of technology. Use the ideas below.

  What type of technology you want to talk about: _____

  _____

  How it works: _____

  _____

  What words you need to describe it: _____

  _____

SPEAK

6 Practise the conversation with your partner. Remember to use infinitives of purpose, the vocabulary from this unit, and phrases from the *Useful language* and *Everyday English* boxes.

CHECK

7 Work with another pair. Listen to their conversation and complete the notes.

  What was the technology? _____

  _____

  How does it work? _____

  _____

WRITING
An article

1 What can you see in the two photos? Can you think of other changes that technology has made at school?

2 Read the article. Does it mention any of your ideas in Exercise 1?

School technology

1 Teaching has changed a lot. **For instance,** in the past, teachers used blackboards and children wrote everything with pen and paper. **What's more,** the only technology in classrooms was a TV or perhaps a cassette player.

2 Today, in contrast, teachers use lots of technology. **For example,** most classrooms have wi-fi. **In addition,** teachers use interactive whiteboards and children use tablets to do exercises or play games. With technology **such as** video chat, classes can work with children in another country. All this makes learning easier and more fun.

3 Some people think that robots might teach children one day. However, I don't think that will happen. Teachers help us learn things, but they take care of us, too. Robots can't do that. The technology may change over time, but the best teachers will always be real people.

3 Read the article again. Are the sentences *T* (true) or *F* (false)?

1 In the past, there was a lot of technology in the classroom. F

2 Children chat to their classmates using video chat. ___

3 It's normal today for classrooms to be connected to the Internet. ___

4 Technology helps children to learn. ___

5 Robots will replace teachers. ___

4 Complete the *Useful language* box with the phrases in **bold** in the article.

Useful language

Giving examples: ¹ For instance,   ² _____
³ _____

Adding more information: ⁴ _____   ⁵ _____

5 Circle the correct words.

1 Tablets are often cheaper than laptops. *What's more, / For example,* they're easier to carry.

2 The first mobile phones could only make calls. *In addition, / For instance,* they were huge.

3 In the future, schools might use technology *such as / what's more* 3D-printing.

Write an article about technology in the home.

PLAN

6 Make notes about technology at home. Think about cooking, cleaning and entertainment. Make notes for your three paragraphs.

1 Technology at home in the past: _____
_____

2 Technology at home today: _____
_____

3 Predictions for the future: _____
_____

WRITE

7 Write your article. Remember to include three paragraphs, past and present tenses, predictions with *will/won't* and *may/might (not)* and phrases from the *Useful language* box.

CHECK

8 Do you ...
• describe technology in the past
• describe technology in the present
• make certain and uncertain predictions for the future?

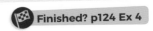 Finished? p124 Ex 4

AROUND THE WORLD

READING
An article

1 Look at the photos. Where do you think this is? What is happening in each photo?

🎧 **2** Read the article. Match photos a–e with paragraphs 1–5.
7.13

Globetrotters
Watch video 7.5
Hello, robots!

- What things do you use robots for?
- What is an android?
- What do you think the future of robots will be?

One morning in the high-tech capital of the world

1 [b] 6.30 am

An alarm buzzes and Seo-yun's phone wakes her up for another day in Seoul, the world's 'tech capital'. In the bathroom, she tells the voice-activated shower to start. Water gushes from the shower but it's too cold. 'Warmer please,' Seo-yun calls out.

2 [ ] 7.20 am

In the kitchen, Dad makes breakfast. While they wait, Seo-yun and her sister, Ji-woo, watch cartoons on the 'family hub' – a huge tablet screen built into the fridge door. They hear a 'ping' – one of Seo-yun's friends has sent a message. Will she go to school on foot or take the bus? Seo-yun asks the family's voice-activated device to check for rain while she checks her travel app to see what the traffic is like.

3 Answer the questions.

1 Where does Seo-yun keep her smartphone at night? _Next to her bed._

2 What doesn't Seo-yun's shower have? _____

3 What is Seo-yun's dad doing while she's watching TV? _____

4 Which two ways of getting to school does Seo-yun think about? _____

5 How does Seo-yun pay for her bus journey? _____

6 What are the other passengers doing on the bus? _____

7 Why is Seo-yun's mum going to Busan? _____

8 Does Ji-woo do gymnastics with Genibo every day? _____

LEARN TO LEARN

Words that describe sounds
There are many English words that sound similar to the sounds they describe.

4 Find and <u>underline</u> words in the article for these sounds.

1 sounds that a smartphone makes (x 3)
   buzz.. , _____ , _____

2 sound effects from a film or cartoon (x 2)
   _____ , _____

3 the sound that a very fast train or other vehicle makes _____

4 the sound of something turning very quickly, for example a robot's wheels _____

5 the sound of water moving fast _____

 5 Look at more words to describe sounds in the box. With a partner, say the words and discuss what sounds you think they describe.

> crack   hiccup   hiss
> miaow   pop   splash   woof

6 Use a dictionary to check the meaning of the words in Exercise 5.

Voice it!

7 Discuss the questions.

1 Does Seo-yun think about other people's feelings? What does she do?

2 Give an example of when you thought about other people's feelings.

---

3 ☐ 8.00 am

Seo-yun has decided to take the bus. There's a beep as she swipes her phone over a sensor when she gets on, and then she takes a seat. On the way, she reads an online comic, and then puts in earphones to enjoy all the bangs, crashes and other sound effects without disturbing other passengers. She doesn't need to worry, though. They're all glued to their screens, too!

4 ☐ 8.10 am

Seo-yun's mum has taken the KTX bullet train to meet colleagues in Busan. The train roars between the two cities at nearly 300 kph. During the journey, she has a video chat with her boss. The journey may soon be much quicker. The government wants to build a new kind of train line called a hyperloop, with trains that zoom along at 1,000 kph.

5 ☐ 8.20 am

Ji-woo has arrived at primary school and the teacher's robot helper, iRobi, comes to Ji-woo with a whir of electric wheels. iRobi marks Ji-woo's attendance and uses face recognition to check her mood. 'Excited?' asks iRobi. Of course. Today Ji-woo might have a gymnastics class with Genibo … the school's robot dog. That's education – Korean style!

Explore it!

Guess the correct answer.

South Korea has the world's fastest …

a internet speeds.   b trains.   c underground.

Find another interesting fact about South Korea. Then write a question for your partner to answer.

OWN IT! The Culture Project Teacher's Resource Bank

VOCABULARY

1 Complete the crossword.

Across

6 Facebook and Instagram are examples of this.

7 A piece of electronic equipment that can connect you to the Internet.

8 You can't touch or see this, but computers can't work without it.

Down

1 Take a file, photo, video, etc. from the Internet and put it onto your device.

2 Put a file from your device onto the Internet.

3 The 'brain' inside your computer or phone.

4 This is when you see and talk to someone using your computer or phone.

5 A short text that you send to someone.

2 Circle the correct words.

1 Eva *caught / went by* the bus outside the bank.

2 Jo travelled from Rome to Pisa *on / by* train.

3 Nina went *by / on* the underground.

4 Zehra got *off / out* the tram at the last stop.

5 Luke *took / caught* a taxi from home and got *out / off* at the airport.

LANGUAGE IN ACTION

3 Complete the sentences with the present perfect form of the verbs in brackets.

1 How annoying! My phone is on silent and I _____ five calls. (miss)

2 You don't need to call a taxi. I _____ one with this app. (book)

3 I don't know what Dina's brother looks like. She _____ any photos of him. (not share)

4 I _____ their new album. I heard it isn't very good. (not download)

4 Circle the correct answers.

1 The bus … leave at 10.02 exactly. It's never late.

   a may   b will   c won't

2 They … be able to do it, but they're trying.

   a can't   b might   c may not

3 Hamza bought some tools … his bike.

   a fix   b to fix   c for fix

4 We haven't got enough ink … the photos.

   a to print   b for to print c for print

Self-assessment

I can use words to talk about communication and technology.	☹	😐	☺
I can use words to talk about getting around.	☹	😐	☺
I can use the present perfect to make affirmative and negative sentences.	☹	😐	☺
I can use *will/won't, may* and *might* to make predictions.	☹	😐	☺
I can use *to* + infinitive to talk about purpose.	☹	😐	☺

LEARN TO LEARN

LEARN TO ... MAKE AND USE FLASHCARDS

You can use flashcards to learn collocations and phrases with prepositions.

1 Match the front and back of the flashcards.

a upload

1 use a messaging _____

2 get into / _____ a car

b app

c for

3 _____ addition

4 _____ / download photos

d get out of

e in

5 _____ instance

device

OWN IT!

2 Match the flashcards in Exercise 1 with the different types of flashcard a–c.
   a a phrase with the preposition missing ☐ ☐
   b a collocation with one word missing ☐
   c opposite collocations with one of them missing ☐ ☐

3 Choose five collocations or phrases with prepositions from Unit 7. Use them to make the different types of flashcards in Exercise 2.

💬 **4** Show the front of your flashcards from Exercise 3 to your partner. Can they guess what is on the back of each flashcard?

   Mobile ... Voice-activated ...

   No, it begins with the letter 'e'.

   Electronic device?   *Yes! That's right!*

💬 **5** Discuss the questions with your partner.
   Which are ...
   1 easier to make, flashcards with phrases with prepositions or flashcards with collocations?
   2 easier to remember with flashcards, phrases with prepositions or collocations?

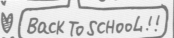

8 HIGH-FLYERS

LEARNING OUTCOMES
I can ...
- understand comments on a web page and a talk about a young inventor
- answer questions in a job interview
- write a competition entry
- understand how to use present perfect for experience, and reflexive and indefinite pronouns
- talk about exceptional jobs and qualities, and achievements
- form people words and make notes
- manage my time and create a timeline.

Start it!

1 Look at the photo. What is the boy learning to do?
2 Before you watch, think of three great human achievements.
3 Why do people say fire is a great human achievement? Watch and check.
4 Think of three personal achievements for you.

Language in action 8.2 p97

Language in action 8.3 p99

Everyday English 8.4 p100

VOCABULARY
Exceptional jobs and qualities

🎧 **1** Match the jobs with the photos. Listen, check and repeat.
8.01

athlete	☐	businessman/businesswoman	☐
composer	☐	inventor	☐
mathematician	☐	scientist	☐
surgeon	1	writer	☐

1
2
3
4
5
6
7
8

🎧 **2** Circle the correct words. Then listen and check.
8.02

1 Olympic athletes like javelin and discus throwers have incredible *creativity* / *strength*.

2 The scientist Albert Einstein was famous for his great *intelligence* / *strength*.

3 At just four years old, Mozart showed a lot of *skill* / *determination* as a composer.

4 J.K. Rowling's *creativity* / *intelligence* as a writer made her famous around the world.

5 Ada Lovelace was an English mathematician. Her *talent* / *creativity* for maths helped to make the modern computer possible.

6 The inventor Thomas Edison worked with a lot of *determination* / *talent* over many years to make his light bulb work.

🛡 LEARN TO LEARN
Word formation: people words

To form nouns describing people, we often add extra letters to a verb or a noun. We sometimes need to change other letters.

3 Complete the table with words in Exercise 1.

Verb / Noun	Extra letters	People word	
invent	-or	1	inventor
compose	-er	2	
write		3	
music	-ian	4	
mathematics		5	
science	-ist	6	
business	-man	7	
	-woman	8	

💬 **4** Test your partner. Ask who …?

Who writes music. | *A composer.*

🎧 **Use it!**

5 Choose three jobs in Exercise 1. Make notes on the special qualities the jobs need.

1 _____
2 _____
3 _____

6 Discuss your ideas.

I think a writer needs a lot of talent and creativity.

Explore it! 🖱

Guess the correct answer.

How old was Louis Braille when he invented his famous alphabet for the blind?

a 10   **b** 15   **c** 25

Find an interesting fact about an amazing achievement. Then write a question for your partner to answer.

READING
Online comments

🗣 **1** **Look at the photos and discuss the questions.**

1 Are the people successful?

2 What do you need to be successful in these areas?

🎧 **2** **Read the online comments. In which area is each person**
8.03 **successful?**

Teenagers taking the world by storm

Yesterday's article about teenagers' achievements has made
a big impression. We've never had so many comments!

1 Krtin Nithiyanandam is only 17, but the intelligence and creativity
of this British schoolboy is amazing. He hasn't studied at
university, but he's done laboratory research into Alzheimer's
disease and is the inventor of a new test for it. He's worked with
Cambridge University scientists and has won awards. Genius!
smartypants 11 m ago

2 Have you ever heard of Mikaila Ulmer? This Texan kid
has won one of the USA's most famous game shows, has
made a fortune as a businesswoman and has even met the
president. She started a lemonade business and entered a
TV competition for entrepreneurs. She won and made a deal
worth millions of dollars. I haven't tried her lemonade, but
it's called BeeSweet. Mikaila gives money to charities that
protect bees and she's even written a book. For a 13-year-old,
she's doing pretty well!
Marion_T 56 m ago

3 We've heard about some incredible prodigies, but how about
Alma Deutscher? She's an incredible 12-year-old musician
from England. Home-schooled, Alma started playing the
piano at two and showed talent even then. She's given
concerts all over the world and she's also a composer. She's
composed pieces for whole orchestras and has even written
an opera. I'm doing my best to learn the violin, so when I saw
Alma on television, I was amazed. With all that skill, I wonder
… has she ever played a wrong note? I doubt it!
Bowfrog 1h 10 m ago

3 Underline the key word(s) or phrase(s)
in the questions. Then write *K* (Krtin),
M (Mikaila) or *A* (Alma).

Who …

1 is <u>under</u> the age of <u>18</u>? <u>K, M, A</u>

2 is from the UK? _____

3 wants to help other people? _____

4 wants to help animals? _____

5 was on TV? _____

6 doesn't go to school? _____

7 met someone famous? _____

4 Find and <u>underline</u> expressions in the
comments with *do* or *make*. Complete
the table with two more examples for
each.

do	make
laboratory research	a big impression

🎤 **Voice it!**

5 **Discuss the questions.**

1 Who do you think has had the most
effect on people's lives: Krtin, Mikaila
or Alma? Why?

2 Do you know of another young
person who has achieved a lot?

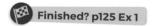
Finished? p125 Ex 1

LANGUAGE IN ACTION
Present perfect for experience

Watch video 8.2
Has Joann ever lost an art competition? Which countries has Joann been to?

I/we/you/they	he/she/it
We'**ve heard** about some incredible prodigies.	He'**s worked** with Cambridge University scientists.
I **haven't tried** her lemonade. We'**ve** ¹ _never_ **had** so many comments.	He **hasn't studied** at university.
Have you ²_____ **heard** of Mikaila Ulmer? Yes, I **have**. / No, I **haven't**.	**Has** she ³_____ **played** a wrong note? Yes, she **has**. / No, she **hasn't**.

> Pronunciation p142

1 Complete the examples in the table above with *ever* or *never*. Use the online comments on page 96 to help you.

⊙ Get it right!

We use an affirmative verb with *never*.

I've never played golf. **NOT** ~~I haven't never played golf.~~

🎧 **2** Maya Flynn is cycling around the world for charity. Complete the interview with the present perfect form of the verbs. Then listen and check.
8.06

PAUL How far ¹_have you cycled_ (you / cycle), Maya?

MAYA ²_____ (I / ride) 10,000 miles so far. I've got another 8,000 to go!

PAUL How many countries ³_____ (you / cross)?

MAYA ⁴_____ (I / be) through three continents so far, and ⁵_____ (I / visit) 12 countries.

PAUL ⁶_____ (you / have) any funny experiences along the way?

MAYA Well, an emu chased me in the Australian outback. ⁷_____ (I / never experience) that before!

PAUL No, not many people have! And how ⁸_____ (your bicycle / be)?

MAYA ⁹_____ (it / not have) any problems at all. It's a great bike.

PAUL So how much money ¹⁰_____ (you / make)?

MAYA ¹¹_____ (I / not reach) my target, but ¹²_____ (I / make) £30,000 so far.

PAUL That's amazing! Good luck with the rest of your journey.

3 Write questions and short answers about the people in the online comments on page 96.

1 Krtin / work / in a laboratory?
Has Krtin worked in a laboratory?
Yes, he has.

2 Mikaila and Alma / be / to university?
_____
_____

3 Marion_T / try / BeeSweet lemonade?
_____
_____

4 Bowfrog / hear / Alma play?
_____
_____

⊙ Use it!

4 Think of questions with the present perfect and *ever*. Use the words in the box.

be on TV	climb a mountain
perform in a concert	raise money for charity
win a competition	win a race

5 Ask and answer your questions.

Have you ever won a competition?

Yes, I have. I won an art competition at primary school.

🎲 **Finished? p125 Ex 2**

VOCABULARY AND LISTENING
Phrasal verbs: achievement

 Use it!

🎧 **1** Listen and repeat the verbs in the box.
8.07 Complete the sentences with the correct form of the verbs. Then match them with the pictures.

> carry on   ~~come up with~~   give up
> keep up with   look up to   set off   set up
> show off   take part in   work out

1 The professor was so happy when he finally
  came up with the answer! _h_

2 Marcus loves to _____ charity races. ____

3 Martha is nearly at the top. She isn't going to
  _____ now! ____

4 The others can't _____ Grandma. ____

5 My brother _____ his own business. ____

6 Thalia really _____ her mum. She wants
  to be just like her one day. ____

7 We've got everything. Let's _____ . ____

8 The maths problem is hard to _____ . ____

9 I don't think I can _____ . Let's rest. ____

10 Aiden likes _____ on the court! ____

 a
 b
 c
 d
 e
 f
 g
 h
 i
 j

2 Write three examples from your own life using phrasal verbs in Exercise 1. Compare with a partner.

1 _____

2 _____

3 _____

> *I wasn't very good at the piano, but I carried on with lessons until I was ten.*

A talk

💬 **3** Discuss the questions.

1 What is the girl doing?   2 What is difficult for her?

🎧 **4** Listen to a talk. Were your ideas right?
8.08

🛡 LEARN TO LEARN

Making notes
Write key words when you listen. Then use your notes to remember the ideas that you heard.

🎧 **5** Listen again and make notes for each heading.
8.08

> Personal details
> [1]Ann Makosinski – Canadian – 20
> _____
>
> Her torch – how it works
> [2]
> Why she thought of the idea
> [3]
> Her achievements
> [4]
> Her E-Drink – how it works
> [5]

💬 **6** Explain how Ann's inventions work. Use your notes in Exercise 5.

LANGUAGE IN ACTION
Reflexive pronouns

Watch video 8.3
What skill should everyone learn? Who does the vlogger say that everyone should know?

Singular	I → ¹myself	you → yourself	he → himself	she → ²_____	it → itself
Plural	we → ³_____	you → ⁴_____	they → themselves		

1 Complete the examples in the table above.

2 Complete the sentences about the talk on page 98 with reflexive pronouns.

  1 Ann taught _herself_ the science that she needed.

  2 Ann's torch switches _____ off.

  3 Ann made the torch _____.

  4 Her inventions don't need batteries. They power _____ in other ways.

  5 If we believe in _____, we can achieve anything.

🎧 3 Match 1–6 with a–f. Then listen and check.
8.09

  1 I surprised _c_

  2 John and I introduced ___

  3 Jane, make sure that you look after ___

  4 Mike has taught ___

  5 You and Vicky should make ___

  6 Stan and Ollie prepared ___

  a ourselves to the new neighbours.

  b themselves well for the match.

  c myself when I did so well in my exams.

  d yourselves some sandwiches for lunch.

  e himself Spanish and French.

  f yourself while I'm away.

Use it!

4 Discuss the questions.

  1 Have you taught yourself a skill? What?

  2 How do you reward yourself when you've done something good?

  3 Where do you imagine yourself in ten years from now?

> *I taught myself to swim when I was eight.*

Indefinite pronouns

People	Things	Places
someone (somebody)	¹_____	somewhere
everyone (everybody)	everything	³_____
no one (nobody)	²_____	nowhere
anyone (anybody)	anything	⁴_____

Ann Makosinski is **someone** I really look up to.
Everything is possible.
No one has thought of these ideas before.

5 Complete the examples in the table above.

🎧 6 Circle the correct words to complete the article. Then listen and check.
8.10

TEENAGER SAILS INTO RECORD BOOKS

Dutch teenager Laura Dekker has become the youngest person ever to sail solo around the world. Laura is only 16 years old. ¹*No one / Anyone* so young has achieved this before. Sailing is ²*something / nothing* all her family are crazy about, and Laura learned ³*anything / everything* she knows about it from her parents. By the time she was 13, there wasn't ⁴*anywhere / nowhere* she couldn't sail by herself. She is now writing a book about her amazing voyage. ⁵*Everyone / Someone* has a dream, and Laura's achievement shows that ⁶*something / nothing* is impossible if you want it enough.

Use it!

7 Complete the sentences. Then compare with your partner.

Everyone in my family likes _____.

I don't know anyone who has _____.

Something I really want to do is _____.

_____ is somewhere I want to visit one day.

🎲 **Finished? p125 Ex 3**

SPEAKING
An interview

🎧 1 **Listen to the conversation. What does Angie want to do?**
8.11

   a learn to cook very well

   b organise a team

JO   ANGIE

JO	So, Angie, why do you want a place on our training scheme?
ANGIE	Well, ¹*I'm passionate about* food. I've taught myself a lot about it, but the training will give me the chance to learn new skills.
JO	So have you ever worked in a kitchen?
ANGIE	Yes, ² _____ working in a restaurant. My grandparents run a restaurant, and I help them at weekends.
JO	Oh really? And what skills have you developed?
ANGIE	³ _____ cooking. But the main thing is ⁴ _____ be a good team player.
JO	That's interesting. Tell me more.
ANGIE	Well, I also help the waiting staff, you see. We take orders from customers and that sort of thing.

🎧 2 **Complete the conversation with the phrases from the *Useful language* box. Then listen and check.**
8.11

> **Useful language**
>
> I'm passionate about …
>
> I've had plenty of experience of …
>
> I've learned how to …
>
> I've learned the basics of …

3 **Look at the *Everyday English* box. Find and underline the phrases in the conversation.**

**Watch video 8.4
Everyday English**

> Tell me more.   that sort of thing
>
> the main thing is   you see

4 **Match the *Everyday English* phrases with their uses.**

You want to …

  1 get more information. _____

  2 refer to similar examples. _____

  3 say your most important point. _____

  4 check the person understands. _____

PLAN

5 **Work with a partner. Make notes on questions to ask in a job interview for one of these jobs.**

> fashion designer   zoo keeper   gardener

_____

_____

SPEAK

6 **Practise the interview with your partner. Remember to use the present perfect to talk about experience, the vocabulary from this unit, and phrases from the *Useful language* and *Everyday English* boxes.**

CHECK

7 **Work with another pair. Listen to their interview and complete the notes.**

What questions did the interviewer ask? _____

_____

What experience does the interviewee have? _____

_____

Should the person get the job? _____

WRITING
A competition entry

1 Read the advert. What sort of competition is this? What is the prize?

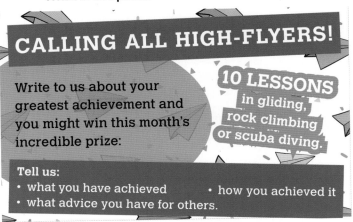

CALLING ALL HIGH-FLYERS!

Write to us about your greatest achievement and you might win this month's incredible prize:

10 LESSONS in gliding, rock climbing or scuba diving.

Tell us:
- what you have achieved
- how you achieved it
- what advice you have for others.

2 Read Ajani's competition entry. What has he achieved?

My name is Ajani. My family came from Afghanistan to live in the UK when I was seven.

My greatest achievement is learning English. When I first came to the UK, I couldn't understand anyone. At school, I couldn't read or write and everything was very difficult. However, after a lot of effort, I've managed to learn English. I've even won a national story writing competition.

How did I manage it? First of all, I had a wonderful teacher called Mrs Connor. She helped me to develop my writing skills. But I also taught myself. I've read plenty of books in English, I've watched lots of lessons on the Internet, and I've practised speaking with friends.

If you want to learn a language, my advice to you is to believe in yourself and never give up.

3 Read Ajani's entry again. Are the sentences *T* (true) or *F* (false)?

1 Ajani is not from England. ___T___
2 He came to the UK by himself. ____
3 His English is still bad. ____
4 He speaks English when he's with friends. ____
5 He thinks that you need determination to succeed. ____

4 Complete the phrases in the *Useful language* box with words from the competition entry.

Useful language

My greatest ¹_____ is …   after a lot of ²_____
How did I ³_____ it?   My ⁴_____ to you is …

5 Rewrite the sentences using the phrases in the *Useful language* box. You might need to write two sentences.

1 I think you should get a teacher. _____
_____

2 The team worked hard and won the prize.
_____

3 I don't know how I learned to fly when I was 15!
_____

4 Learning French was the best thing I have done.
_____

Write a competition entry.

PLAN

6 Make notes about one of your achievements.
1 Introduce yourself: _____
2 Explain the achievement: _____
_____
3 Explain how you achieved it: _____
_____
4 Give advice for other people: _____

WRITE

7 Write your competition entry. Remember to include the present perfect, reflexive pronouns, vocabulary from this unit and phrases from the *Useful language* box.

CHECK

8 Do you …
- have four paragraphs?
- explain your achievement clearly?
- give useful advice?

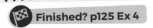
Finished? p125 Ex 4

THE DESIGN AND TECHNOLOGY PROJECT

A timeline

1 **Read texts 1–6 on the timeline quickly. Then match them with the pictures A–F.**

1 [C]   2 [ ]   3 [ ]   4 [ ]   5 [ ]   6 [ ]

2 **For each question, choose the correct inventor. Some questions have more than one answer.**

Which inventor or inventors …

1 worked with a brother? _d, f_
2 studied how birds fly? _____
3 had an accident? _____
4 wasn't European? _____
5 didn't fly the machine himself? _____
6 designed an aircraft with an engine? _____

a Eilmer of Malmesbury
b Leonardo da Vinci
c Denis Bolor
d Joseph-Michel Montgolfier
e Jules Giffard
f Orville Wright

How to manage your time

3 **Look at some ideas to think about before you start a project. Tick (✓) the ideas connected to planning your time.**

a Decide on a topic for the project. [ ]
b Think about all the tasks you need to do in the time available. [ ]
c Prioritise tasks – decide what's most and least important. [ ]
d Include some extra time. [ ]
e Decide who will do what. [ ]
f Set long-term deadlines. [ ]
g Set short-term deadlines. [ ]
h Review your project regularly to see if you are keeping to your deadlines. [ ]

🎧 8.12 **4** **Listen to two students planning a project. Which ideas in Exercise 3 do they talk about?**

_____, _____, _____, _____, _____

1

Eilmer of Malmesbury, England, has had a great idea. He ties himself to a pair of wings and jumps off the top of a tower. Eilmer flies for 200 metres. No one has ever flown so far. However, Eilmer hasn't thought about the landing! He hurts himself badly, but also gets himself a place in the history books.

● 1010

5

French engineer Jules Giffard connects a steam engine to a huge balloon. It's the first 'airship'. People have never seen anything like it before. It's the first aircraft that someone can steer. However, the first time Giffard sets off in his airship, it flies round in circles. He can't steer it against the strong Paris winds!

● 1852

E

● 1903

6

It's 10.35 am on 17 December. American engineer Orville Wright has lifted himself into the air. He's flying the Wright Flyer, a motor-powered aeroplane he designed with his brother Wilbur. Orville keeps the Flyer in the air for 12 seconds and travels 37 metres. It isn't a long-distance flight, but it has changed the world forever.

HIGH (AND NOT SO HIGH) ACHIEVERS
THE EARLY HISTORY OF FLIGHT

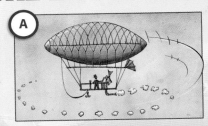

A

2 The brilliant Italian scientist and inventor Leonardo da Vinci has looked into how birds fly. Using his discoveries, he designs the world's first flying machine – the Ornithopter. But he has the intelligence not to try it himself! Later, other people try out similar designs, but no one gets very far.

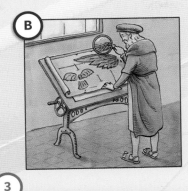

B

3 Frenchman Denis Bolor has come up with his own flying machine that uses wings with springs. Poor Bolor tries to show off his idea, but kills himself when the springs break.

1485

C

1536

1783

D

4 French businessman Joseph-Michel Montgolfier and his brother, Jacques-Étienne, have invented the world's first hot-air balloon. Now they make a second flight with passengers. But they don't put themselves on board. The three lucky passengers are a hen, a duck and a sheep!

F

PLAN

5 Work in groups. Choose one of the inventions in the box or choose your own. Then complete the steps below.

> the bicycle   the computer
> the Internet   the skyscraper

- Decide what tasks you need to do to complete your timeline and how long each will take.
- Set long-term and short-term deadlines and include some extra time.
- Decide who will do each task.
- Research the information you need.
- Find or make pictures for your timeline.

PRESENT

6 Display your timeline on your classroom wall. Remember to include important dates, people and events, interesting pictures and the tips in *How to* manage your time.

CHECK

7 Look at your classmates' timelines. Which ones have interesting facts?

VOCABULARY

1 Complete the sentences with the words for jobs and qualities.

1 She's going to succeed. She's got plenty of d_____ .

2 You need a lot of s_____ to be a concert pianist.

3 C_____ is important if you want to be a good designer.

4 I'm so tired. I don't have the s_____ to stand up.

5 Nick has written some brilliant songs. I think he'll be a professional c_____ .

6 I am terrible at maths. I could never be a m_____ !

7 I could be an i_____ . I have lots of ideas for new machines.

2 Complete the sentences with words from both boxes. Use the correct form of the verbs. Use some words more than once.

| come | give | keep | set | work |

| off | out | up | with |

1 I did ballet for three years, but I _____ it _____ because I wasn't good at it.

2 Mira is running too fast for me. I can't _____ her.

3 Next week, I'm going to _____ on a journey across Europe.

4 Do you know the answer? I can't _____ it _____ .

5 Amol has _____ a brilliant idea for our team project.

LANGUAGE IN ACTION

3 Complete the questions with *ever* and the verbs in the box. Then write the short answers.

| have | ride | see | try | visit |

1 A _____ you _____ a snake?
  B _____ . We saw one in our garden.

2 A _____ your brother _____ an accident in his car?
  B _____ . He's a very careful driver.

3 A _____ your parents _____ the USA?
  B _____ . They went there six years ago.

4 A _____ you _____ to invent something?
  B _____ . But it wasn't successful!

5 A _____ Fiona _____ a horse?
  B _____ . Unfortunately, she fell off!

4 Circle the correct words.

1 Dan set up a business *themselves / himself*.

2 We built our house *myself / ourselves*.

3 You won't achieve *anything / anywhere* if you don't try.

4 This computer has taught *itself / myself* to play chess.

5 Is there *no one / anyone* who knows Patrick's address?

Self-assessment

I can use words to talk about exceptional jobs and qualities.	☹	😐	☺
I can use phrasal verbs to talk about achievement.	☹	😐	☺
I can use the present perfect to talk about experience.	☹	😐	☺
I can use reflexive pronouns.	☹	😐	☺
I can use indefinite pronouns.	☹	😐	☺

LEARN TO ... MAKE A VOCABULARY STUDY PLAN

You can learn vocabulary better by studying it more than once. A study plan can help you do this.

1 Do the quiz. Circle your answers.

Do you need a vocabulary study plan?
FIND OUT!

Do you ...

1 write new vocabulary in your notebook?
 always / sometimes / never

2 use flashcards to learn vocabulary?
 always / sometimes / never

3 look at your vocabulary notes when you do your homework?
 always / sometimes / never

4 study your vocabulary notes before a test?
 always / sometimes / never

5 study your vocabulary notes more than three times a week?
 always / sometimes / never

Results

always = **2 points**   *sometimes* = **1 point**   *never* = **0 point**

8–10: Well done! You study vocabulary well, but why not try a new study plan?

4–7: Not bad, but a study plan can help you.

0–3: Oh, dear! You really need a study plan!

2 Ask your partner the quiz questions. <u>Underline</u> their answers.

3 Find out your score. Do you agree with what it says about you? Discuss the results with a partner.

4 Match 1–3 with a–c. Which sentence surprises you most? Discuss with your partner.

1 We remember vocabulary better when we study it once and ☐

2 When you use flashcards to learn vocabulary, ☐

3 It's necessary to see, hear or say a word ☐

a 17 times before we remember it well.

b then a few days later (but not the next day).

c you remember it better.

5 Make a list of eight words from this unit that you want to learn. Make flashcards.

_____ _____ _____ _____

_____ _____ _____ _____

OWN IT!

6 Follow steps 1–5 to make a ten-day vocabulary study plan.

1 Write the dates on the plan, starting with tomorrow's date.

2 On the days in yellow, test yourself with your flashcards.

3 On the other days, study the list of words in Exercise 5 for at least five minutes.

4 When you finish studying each day, write 'Yes!' in the 'Done?' box.

5 On day 11, answer the question and circle 'a lot' or 'a bit'.

Day	1	2	3	4	5	6	7	8	9	10	How much has the plan helped me learn vocabulary? *a lot / a bit*
Date											
Done?											

9

SHOW YOUR MOVES

LEARNING OUTCOMES
I can ...
- understand texts about music
- make polite refusals
- write a review
- understand how to use *going to*, *will*, the present continuous for the future and the present simple for the future
- talk about and describe musical instruments and genres, and dance styles
- recognise stress patterns, distinguish between speakers and use referencing.

▶ **Start it!**

1 Look at the photo. What do you think the man is doing?

2 Before you watch, how does music make you feel?

3 How do people who can't hear enjoy music? Watch and check.

4 What instruments do you play or do you want to play?

Watch video 9.1

Language in Action 9.2

p109

Language in Action 9.3

p111

Everyday English 9.4

p112

Globetrotters 9.5

p114

VOCABULARY
Musical instruments and genres

🎧 9.01 **1** Match the words in the boxes with the musical instruments and genres (1–14) in the pictures. Listen, check and repeat.

classical	1	folk	☐	hip-hop	☐
jazz	☐	reggae	☐	rock	☐

bass	☐	drums	☐
guitar	☐	keyboard	☐
microphone	☐	saxophone	☐
trumpet	☐	violin	☐

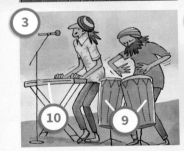

💬 **2** How many other musical instruments and genres can you think of?

◉ **Get it right!**

We say *play football*, *tennis*, *golf*, etc.
But we say *play **the** piano*, **the** *guitar*, **the** *trumpet*, etc.

🛡 LEARN TO LEARN
Stress patterns

It's important to learn which syllable is stressed when you learn a new word.

🎧 9.02 **3** Complete the table with words in Exercise 1. Then listen and check. Can you add one more word to each group?

O	folk,
Oo	
oO	
Ooo	classical,
ooO	

💬 **4** Take turns to clap the rhythm of a word in Exercise 1. Your partner guesses the word.

🔵 **Use it!**

5 Discuss the questions.
1 What kind of music do you like listening to?
2 Can you or your friends or family play a musical instrument? Which one?
3 Which instruments do you like the sound of?

Explore it! 🖱

Guess the correct answer.

Chicago rapper, Twista, is one of the fastest rappers in the world. What's the fastest he can rap?

a 10 syllables per second
b 20 syllables per second
c 30 syllables per second

Find an interesting fact about music. Then write a question for your partner to answer.

READING
An events guide

1 Look at the photos of four musicians. What sort of music do you think they play?

9.03 2 Read the events guide. Match musicians 1–4 with the genres that they are going to perform.

pop ☐ blues ☐ raga ☐
country and western ☐

3 Match concerts A–D with these features. Sometimes there is more than one concert.

1 A   only one performer
2 ___ includes an electronic instrument
3 ___ free for some people
4 ___ has more than two performers
5 ___ includes a violin
6 ___ starts before eight o'clock
7 ___ cheaper for people at university
8 ___ starts the latest

4 Find adjectives in the guide that mean:

1 alone   solo
2 very excited   _____
3 famous   _____
4 very unusual   _____
5 surprising   _____
6 talented   _____

 Voice it!

5 Put the concerts in the events guide in order, from most interesting to least interesting. Explain your choices to your partner.

1 ANGUS 'THE BEARD' BEARDSLEY

2 BUNNY SCRAGGS

3 DR JAY

4 JANET GLYNDEBOURNE

WATERSIDE ARTS CENTRE What's on at the Waterside

A   Tuesday 8 pm
Bunny Scraggs
£8.00, £3.00 (student discount)

We think this show will surprise reggae fans. The Dubster Brothers' bassist also plays blues piano, and he's going to share that talent tonight. In this solo performance, Bunny's going to play and sing his favourite blues classics. However, if you want to hear some of the Dubster Brothers' hits, we're sure Bunny won't disappoint!

B   Thursday 7 pm
Janet Glyndebourne and the Donuts
£5, no charge for under 16s

We're thrilled to welcome Janet Glyndebourne to Waterside. However, the well-known opera star isn't going to sing Mozart. Instead, she's going to join Kim Green on synthesiser and Bod on percussion, and they're going to play a concert of pure pop. We're sure it will be a great evening!

C   Saturday 7.30 pm
Dr Jay and the Rodeo Band
£10.00, £4.00 (student discount)

For one night only, hip-hop artist Dr Jay is going to lead country and western favourites the Rodeo Band (Helen Smith on banjo and vocals, Liam Jones on double bass, Lucy-Anne Flynn on violin). Are you really going to miss this unique event? We're sure you won't want to!

D   Sunday 9.30 pm
Angus Beardsley plays raga
£15.00, £7.00

Rock legends Axel Heads have announced that they aren't going to tour again. Their fans will miss them, but we have some unexpected news! The band's bass player, Angus 'The Beard' Beardsley, is also a gifted violinist. On Saturday he's going to team up with sitar player Jagjit Rakha to perform Indian raga. But is 'The Beard' going to sing in Hindi, too? Come and find out!

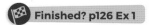 **Finished? p126 Ex 1**

LANGUAGE IN ACTION
going to

Watch video 9.2
Which music festival is Fiona going to? What music is Evita going to listen to?

I/he/she/it		you/we/they	
He¹ _'s going to_ **share** that talent tonight.		They² _____ **play** a concert of pure pop.	
Janet **isn't going to sing** Mozart.		Axel Heads ³_____ **tour** again.	
⁴_____ 'The Beard' _____ **sing** in Hindi?		**Are** you really **going to miss** this unique event?	

1 Complete the examples in the table above with the correct form of *going to*. Use the events guide on page 108 to help you.

2 Complete the sentences about the events guide with the correct form of *going to*.

  1 The concerts _aren't going to start_ (not start) before 7 pm.

  2 Two concerts _____ (take) place at the weekend.

  3 Bunny Scraggs _____ (play) blues piano.

  4 Janet Glyndebourne _____ (not perform) classical music.

3 Complete the conversation with the correct form of *going to*. Then listen and check.
9.04

AVA Hi, Josh. ¹ _Are you going to go_ (you / go) out tomorrow evening?

JOSH No, I'm not in the mood. ²_____ (I / stay) at home and watch TV instead. What about you?

AVA Yeah. Dr Jay is at the Waterside. ³_____ (I / not miss) that.

JOSH Wow! Really?

AVA Yeah, really. ⁴_____ (I / buy) my ticket this morning.

JOSH Hmm. Sounds interesting. ⁵_____ (Aneta / join) you?

AVA Aneta? ⁶_____ (she / not come). She can't stand Dr Jay. Why don't you come?

JOSH OK, you've convinced me. But how ⁷_____ (we / get) there?

  ⁸_____ (we / not walk), are we?

AVA ⁹_____ (my dad / give) us a lift.

will and going to

will for ¹ _____	going to for ² _____
We're sure it **will be** a great evening!	Bunny**'s going to play** his favourite blues classics.

4 Complete the headings in the table above with *intentions* or *predictions*.

5 Decide if these sentences are *P* (predictions) or *I* (intentions). Then complete the sentences and check your answers on page 108.

  1 We think this show __will__ surprise reggae fans. _P_

  2 We're sure Bunny _____ disappoint! __

  3 She _____ join Kim Green. __

  4 Dr Jay _____ lead the Rodeo Band. __

6 Complete Lia's message to Max. Use the verbs in the box with *going to* or *will*.

  be   buy   fail   g̶o̶   like   not be able   play

Hey Max. ¹ _Are you_ and Mo _going to go_ to Jo's party? I think it ²_____ fun. Jo's brother has a band and they ³_____ at the party. I'm sure you ⁴_____ them.
⁵_____ you _____ tickets for the Z Men concert? I probably ⁶_____ to go. We've got a test that week, and I ⁷_____ it if I don't study.

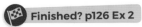**Use it!**

7 Tell your partner about your intentions and predictions for the weekend.

Finished? p126 Ex 2

VOCABULARY AND LISTENING
Dance styles

1 Match the words in the box with the photos.
Listen, check and repeat.
9.05

ballet dancing	☐	ballroom dancing	1
breakdance	☐	country dancing	☐
disco dancing	☐	modern dance	☐
salsa dancing	☐	swing	☐
tap dancing	☐	zumba	☐

Use it!

2 **Discuss the dance styles in Exercise 1.**
1 What type of music accompanies the styles?
2 What do people usually wear for these styles?
3 Which dance style do you think looks best? Why?

A discussion

3 **Listen to a conversation between four students.**
What are they talking about?
9.06
a A show they have seen
b A show they are planning

LEARN TO LEARN

Distinguishing between speakers
When you listen to a group of people speaking, it can be difficult to understand who says what. Listen for names and note them down. For each person, consider these things:

- Are they male or female?
- Are they old or young?
- Can you hear an accent? Are they a native speaker or a non-native speaker?

4 **Listen again and match the people with the tasks.**
9.06

1	Imogen	a	recording the show
2	Marta	b	writing the programme
3	Adam	c	organising the music
4	Jack	d	putting out the seats

Voice it!

5 **Discuss the questions.**
1 Have you ever helped organise a school show or a similar event?
2 What do you think is the most difficult part of organising a show?

LANGUAGE IN ACTION
Present continuous for future

Watch video 9.3
What is Paulo doing on Saturday night? What time does the movie begin?

Present continuous for future plans

I ¹_____ **writing** the programme.
I ²_____ **not doing** anything on Friday afternoon.
³_____ you **recording** the show, Adam?

> Pronunciation p142

1 Complete the examples in the table above.

2 Correct the sentences about the conversation between Imogen and her friends.

  1 The teachers are having a party on Friday afternoon.
    They aren't having a party. They're having a meeting.

  2 The show is taking place in a theatre. _____

  3 Jack is recording the show on his phone. _____

  4 They're using a live band for the show. _____

🎧 3 Complete Lilia's post with the present continuous form of the verbs in the box. Then listen and check.
9.08

| bring come leave meet not do perform play ~~return~~ |

Thank you, Oxford! You were a fabulous audience last night! We¹ *'re returning* in September, so I hope we'll see some of you again. Later today, we ²_____ for Edinburgh. We ³_____ a new play there, called *The Bell*, and I ⁴_____ a girl who has the power to see the future. Hey, Edinburgh! If you ⁵_____ anything on Friday night, come along. Guess who ⁶_____ to see us on our first night – Emma Watson! She ⁷_____ her friends, and we ⁸_____ them backstage after the performance. Wow!

Present simple for future

Present simple for scheduled events

It ¹_____ (begin) at seven thirty.
The doors ²_____ (not open) until 7 o'clock.
What time ³_____ the show _____ (start)?

4 Complete the examples in the table above with the correct form of the verbs in brackets.

5 Complete sentences 1–4 using the present simple for the future.

DANCE-FEST

Barnsley Dance Festival Saturday 21 June

12.30–2.00: African Beat Workshop
Learn traditional African dances.

3.00–4.00: The Langley Dance School
Watch the world's favourite ballet, *Swan Lake*.

6.15–7.00: Tarantella Talk
Gianna Romano gives a talk about one of Italy's most famous dances.

7.30–9.00: The Bronx River Combo
See this New York street dance group doing hip-hop, krumping and more.

| end last ~~start~~ take |

1 The festival *starts* at lunchtime.

2 African Beat _____ place first.

3 The ballet performance _____ for more than an hour.

4 The Bronx River Combo's performance _____ until 9 pm.

🔵 **Use it!**

6 Ask and answer the questions about each event at Dance-Fest.

  1 What time does it start and finish?

  2 What is happening in the event?

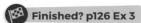 **Finished? p126 Ex 3**

SPEAKING
Making polite refusals

1 Listen to the conversation. What event is Harry going to? Why can't Jess go? 🎧 9.09

HARRY **JESS**

HARRY Hi, Jess. I'm going to book tickets for the jazz festival this Saturday afternoon. ¹*Do you fancy* coming along?

JESS ² _____ my cousin Helen's visiting me and I'll be with her all day long.

HARRY ³ _____ join us if she wants.

JESS That's really kind of you, Harry, but ⁴ _____ Helen can't stand jazz!

HARRY Oh, that's a pity. Look, they're playing for two nights. What are you up to on Friday? ⁵ _____ come then instead?

JESS Hmm. What time does it start?

HARRY 7.30.

JESS Oh, that's no good either, Harry. I've got a guitar lesson and it starts at 7.15.

HARRY OK. Never mind, Jess. Maybe another time.

JESS Sure. ⁶ _____ . I'm sure it'll be a great concert.

2 Complete the conversation with phrases from the *Useful language* box. Then listen and check. 🎧 9.09

> **Useful Language**
>
> Do you fancy …?   I'd love to, but …
>
> I'm afraid …   (She's) welcome to …
>
> Thanks for asking, though   Would you like to …?

3 Look at the *Everyday English* box. Find and <u>underline</u> the phrases in the conversation.

Watch video 9.4 Everyday English

> all day long   Never mind.   That's a pity.
> That's no good   What are you up to?

4 Match the phrases in the *Everyday English* box with their meanings.

1 That isn't convenient. _____
2 It doesn't matter. _____
3 for the whole day _____
4 That's sad. _____
5 What plans have you got? _____

PLAN

5 Work with a partner. Think of an event to go to and reasons why one of you can't go.

SPEAK

6 Practise the conversation with your partner. Remember to include *going to*, *will* , the present simple and present continuous, the vocabulary from this unit, and phrases from the *Useful language* and *Everyday English* boxes.

CHECK

7 Work with another pair. Listen to their conversation and complete the notes.

What event do they decide on? _____

_____

Why can't one of them go? _____

_____

WRITING
A review

1 Read the review quickly. Which dance styles can you see in this show?

'Hiplet' – a new dance experience!

Crash Dance Crew are a dance group from Chicago. Their show, *City Dreams*, tells the story of three teenagers who have come to the city to make a new life for themselves. The show is a unique mix of hip-hop and ballet called hiplet. Three musicians on keyboards, vocals and turntable play a mix of rap and electro funk.

It's an action-packed story, but there are some funny moments, too.

The costumes are beautiful and I was impressed by the music. However, the highlight of the show is the dancing. The mix of styles works well. On the downside, tickets are expensive and there's no student discount.

Crash Dance Crew play at the Nottingham Malthouse Theatre next week. After that, they're touring other cities in the UK. All in all, if you love dance, this superb show is a must-see.

2 Read the review again and correct these sentences.

1 The performers are from Nottingham.

The performers are from Chigago.

2 An orchestra plays the music for the show.

3 The writer liked the music most.

4 Tickets are cheaper for students.

5 The show is only happening in Nottingham.

3 In a review, it's a good idea to use lots of adjectives. Find and underline all the adjectives in the dance show review. Discuss with a partner what they describe.

4 Find and underline the *Useful language* phrases in the review. Match 1–5 with the phrases.

1 The best part was
2 I loved
3 It was disappointing that
4 In summary
5 Fans of (dance) will love this

Useful Language

All in all ☐
If you love (dance), this (show) is a must-see. ☐
I was impressed by … ☐
On the downside ☐
The highlight of the show is … ☐

Write a review of a concert or show.

PLAN

5 Think about a concert or a show you have seen. Make notes about these things.

1 A general description of the show
2 Details about the dancing, music, costumes, etc. and what you liked/didn't like
3 A summary of your opinion

WRITE

6 Write your review. Remember to use adjectives, the present simple to describe the show, the past simple for your opinion and phrases from the *Useful language* box.

CHECK

Do you …

• use three paragraphs?
• say what you liked and didn't like?
• summarise your opinions at the end?

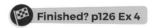 **Finished? p126 Ex 4**

AROUND THE WORLD

READING
A travel article

💬 **1** **Look at the photos and discuss the questions.**
1 What sort of dance do they show?
2 What else do you know about this dance?
3 What more would you like to know about it?

Globetrotters
Watch video 9.5
The Schuhplattler

- Which dances from other countries do you know?
- Where is the *Schuhplattler* dance from?
- Which traditional dances from your own country do you know?

🎧 **2** **Read the article. Does it mention any of**
9.10 **your ideas in Exercise 1?**

3 **Read the article again and answer the questions.**
1 How long does the *Festival De Jerez* last? _Two weeks_
2 Who goes to the festival?
_____
_____
3 What can you do at the festival?
_____
_____
4 What traditions does flamenco come from?
_____
_____
5 When did flamenco performers start using guitars? _____
6 What mistake do people often make about flamenco? _____
7 What part of a flamenco performance can the audience take part in? _____
_____

Festival de Jerez:
a flamenco heaven
by Dan Philips

Every year the Spanish city of Jerez puts on a festival of flamenco dance. This year's festival begins tomorrow and lasts for two wonderful weeks. For me, and flamenco fans around the world, ¹it's the highlight of the year. People from over 30 different countries will turn up here, all crazy about flamenco.

Every day, there are performances of flamenco. ²Some take place in the beautiful Villamarta Theatre, but most happen in the small flamenco clubs all around Jerez, known as *peñas*. And if you're keen to take it up yourself, the greatest flamenco teachers from around the world are going to give classes.

The festival begins on 23 February and ends on 10 March. Don't miss out!

SOME HISTORY

Flamenco is typically Spanish, but it has a long international history. Over five centuries ago, the Roma came to Europe from India and brought their traditional music. ³Their traditions mixed with local traditions from the south of Spain and ⁴those of Jewish and North African immigrants, and the result was flamenco.

The 19th century was the 'golden age' of flamenco. The first flamenco schools opened ⁵then, in Seville, Cadiz and Jerez. Performers began to use guitars, and dance became more important. Flamenco became the art we know today.

A GUIDE FOR BEGINNERS

Instruments: The two most important of ⁶these are the guitar and the castanets, but you might also see performances with trumpets, violins or even a whole orchestra.

Songs: People often think that flamenco is only dancing. In fact, the songs, called *cante*, are the real heart of it. The words are often by Spain's most famous poets.

Dance: *Zapateado* is the special dance that flamenco dancers do. They stamp their feet and click their castanets in fast, complicated rhythms. Nobody nods off during a flamenco concert!

Jaleo: This is the hand-clapping and shouting that make flamenco so exciting. The clapping, called *palmas*, is much more difficult to do than it looks. But anyone can join in the shouting, so don't be shy!

 **LEARN TO LEARN**

Referencing

Writers often use words such as *this* and *that* to refer back to something they have already mentioned in the text.

4 What do <u>underlined</u> words 1–6 in the article refer to?

1 ___the festival___   4 _____

2 _____   5 _____

3 _____   6 _____

5 Find and underline six phrasal verbs in the article with the verbs below. Complete the sentences using the correct form.

> join ~~miss~~ nod put take turn

1 Buy tickets early so you don't ___miss out___.

2 My mum _____ flamenco guitar last year.

3 They _____ the biggest concerts in the Villamarta Theatre.

4 This music is so boring – it's making me _____.

5 We _____ late and couldn't get into the concert.

6 Would you like to _____ the dance with us?

🔊 **Voice it!**

6 Discuss the questions.

1 What different cultures are there where you live?

2 Why is it important to understand other cultures?

Explore it! 🖱

Guess the correct answer.

Jerez is also home to a world-famous … school.

a rock–climbing **b** film **c** horse–riding

Find three more interesting facts about Spanish traditions. Choose your favourite fact and write a question for your partner to answer.

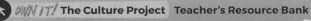

🖱 *OWN IT!* **The Culture Project** Teacher's Resource Bank

VOCABULARY

1 Write the names of the musical instruments.

1 _____
2 _____
3 _____
4 _____
5 _____
6 _____

2 Complete the dance styles.

1 _ _ e a _ _ a _ _ e
2 _ a _ _ a _ a _ _ i _ _
3 _ _ i _ _
4 _ a _ _ _ o o _ _ a _ _ i _ _
5 _ a _ _ e _ _ a _ _ i _ _
6 _ i _ _ o _ a _ _ i _ _

LANGUAGE IN ACTION

3 Complete the sentences with the verbs in the box. Use the correct form of *going to* or *will*.

| be   enjoy   learn   meet   not be |
| not visit   show   tour |

1 My favourite band _____ the UK, but it probably _____ my town.
2 Elif thinks we _____ able to learn these dance steps, but we _____ her that we can.
3 James has decided he _____ the piano, and I think he _____ it.
4 I _____ Rosie at the salsa class, but I'm sure she _____ late, as usual!

4 Complete the sentences with the present simple or present continuous form of the verbs.

1 Adriana _____ (bring) her guitar to the party on Saturday.
2 We need to hurry. The show _____ (start) in five minutes.
3 Sara and Jez _____ (not come) to the theatre tomorrow. They've got too much homework.
4 There's a bus that _____ (get) to the concert hall at 7.15.
5 The concert _____ (not end) until 11 o'clock. That's quite late.
6 What _____ you _____ (do) tomorrow night? Do you want to come to my concert?

Self-assessment

I can use words to talk about musical instruments and genres. 😕 😐 🙂

I can use words to talk about dance styles. 😕 😐 🙂

I can use *will* and *going to* to talk about predictions and intentions. 😕 😐 🙂

I can use the present continuous and the present simple for the future. 😕 😐 🙂

LEARN TO … PRACTISE YOUR ENGLISH DURING THE HOLIDAYS

It's important to practise English during the holidays, especially when the holidays are long.

1 Read the conversation between Egor and Polina. Then circle the correct answers.

> **EGOR** Two months without English classes!
>
> **POLINA** But if we don't practise, we'll forget everything.
>
> POLINA   EGOR
>
> **EGOR** I don't want that! We've learned a lot this year.
>
> **POLINA** Well, why don't we make a list of things we can do in English during the holidays.
>
> **EGOR** That's a great idea!

1 They're speaking … the school year.
   a during   b at the end of

2 They don't want to … their English.
   a forget   b use

3 They're going to …
   a ask for help.   b think of ways to practise.

2 Egor and Polina begin their list. What do ideas 1–6 practise? Write *S* (speaking), *L* (listening), *R* (reading) or *W* (writing).

> **Things to do in English over the summer**
>
> 1 Podcasts (easy ones on English online) __L__
> 2 Keep a scrapbook of places we visit. ____ , ____
> 3 Change the language of our phone apps to English. ____
> 4 Pay attention to station and airport announcements in English when we travel. ____
> 5 Send messages to each other in English! ____ , ____
> 6 Help a tourist who speaks English. ____ , ____
> 7 _____
> 8 _____
> 9 _____
> 10 _____

3 Work in pairs. Think of four more ways to practise English during the holidays – one each for speaking, listening, reading and writing. Write them in Egor and Polina's list (7–10).

OWN IT!

4 Make a plan for practising English during the holidays.

1 Choose four of the ten ideas from the list and write them in the table (1–4).

2 Decide when or how often you are going to do them. Complete 5–8.

	Idea	When? / How often?
Speaking	Record a voice message for my aunt in English.	Once a week.
Listening	Listen to airport announcements.	When I fly to see my cousin.
Speaking	1 _____	5 _____
Listening	2 _____	6 _____
Reading	3 _____	7 _____
Writing	4 _____	8 _____

5 Tell your partner what you're going to do. Are there any things you can do together?

> *For speaking, I'm going to record a voice message for my aunt once a week.*

> *Why don't you record one for me too? Then I can send you one back!*

> *Great idea! That will help our listening as well!*

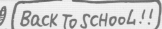

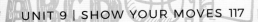

A	B	C	D	E	F	G	H	I	J	K	L	M
✦	♥	☞	☾	➾	⊛	◯	✳	★	☎	♣	✎	✪

N	O	P	Q	R	S	T	U	V	W	X	Y	Z
➥	❖	✖	✢	❀	✈	❄	✠	▨	●	✂	✆	➤

1 What do they like watching?
Use the code and write the TV shows.

1 Miriam — *sports shows*
2 Ahmed — _____
3 Lidia and Ryan — _____
4 Mya's parents — _____
5 Sara's brother — _____

2 Write sentences about four more differences.

In A, Emma is talking on her phone. In B she's listening to music.

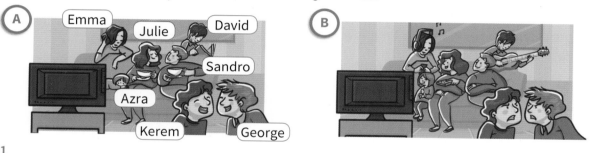

1 _____
2 _____
3 _____
4 _____

3 Read the clues and write the answers.

1 The director is shouting at the actors. Usually he's very quiet! How is he speaking? _loudly_
2 I'm reading this book and it's taking me a long time. How am I reading? _____
3 My teacher says I'm a great student! How am I doing? _____
4 I'm very busy. I'm doing all my homework before lunchtime. How am I working? _____
5 I always understand my science teacher. How does she explain things? _____

4 Complete the puzzle and find the mystery word.

1 c o s t u m e
2
3
4
5
6

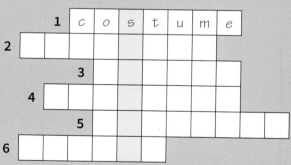

make-up …

sound …

camera …

2 FINISHED?

1 Circle eight weather words.

P	E	T	V	W	A	R	M	C
S	H	O	C	E	G	H	K	L
N	D	H	O	T	O	I	R	O
O	F	E	L	O	L	C	U	U
W	I	N	D	Y	P	Y	I	D
Y	P	P	O	S	U	N	N	Y

2 Put the letters in order to make eight past simple verbs. Then write the infinitive form of the verbs.

1) h o t t g u h

thought - think

2) t e a

3) m a s w

4) r a k d n

5) a d e r h

6) k o t o

3 Find four sentences in the grid by connecting the words. You can move in any direction: →←↑↓↖↗↙↘.

There	→ weren't	There	were	a	kitchen
were	any ↓	in	a	some	There
There	students	sofa	the	was	children
wasn't	in	wallet.	classroom.	a	in
the	any	room.	the	nice	the
a	living	money	in	park.	some

4 Look at the box for one minute. Then cover it and write all the useful objects you can remember.

fork,

1 Circle the letters and write the adjectives of feeling.

1

(w)	x	c
s	(o)	(d)
y	(r)	(e)
e	(r)	(i)

worried

2

e	o	l
r	n	s
l	e	r
y	s	v

_____

3

u	s	u
n	e	o
t	r	v
i	d	e

_____

4

e	d	r
y	i	f
r	g	a
o	n	s

_____

5

e	l	u
u	s	p
m	e	r
t	b	a

_____

2 Look at the picture for one minute. Then close your book and write as many sentences about the people as you can in your notebook.

Tilly and Milly

Theo

Mr and Mrs Lopez

Grandma

What were they doing when the storm started?

Tilly and Milly were sitting up in their beds.

3 Find all the words in the same colour to make five questions. Then write and answer the questions in your notebook.

What	Did you go	selfies	at 10 pm
Were you	two days ago	were you sitting	yesterday
shopping	were you doing	with friends	for an exam
How many	last Saturday	did you take	in your last class
Who	revising	next to	last night

What were you doing at 10 pm last night?

4 Complete 1–8 with prepositions of movement. Then put the letters in circles in order to find out what ice cream Milo had (9).

Milo went ¹o u t o f his house. He walked ² _____ ◯ the street and he walked ³ ___ ◯ _____ the bus stop. Then he went ⁴ _____ ◯ _____ the road. He walked ⁵ _____ the steps and he went ⁶ ___ ◯ _____ the bridge. Then he went ⁷ _ ◯ _ the steps on the other side and ⁸ ___ ◯ _____ the park. Finally, he stopped to buy some ⁹ _____ ice cream!

1 Circle ten money verbs.

A	O	S	E	L	L	C	N	J	D
W	C	O	F	R	E	A	S	V	O
B	O	R	R	O	W	Y	P	Y	C
S	S	Y	G	W	R	P	E	U	H
C	T	E	H	E	A	R	N	I	A
P	L	P	N	H	N	T	D	S	N
D	S	A	V	E	W	M	R	N	G
N	V	Y	D	P	L	E	N	D	E

2 Read the information and complete the table about famous shopping malls.

- The West Edmonton Mall is 27 years older than the Dubai Mall.
- The West Edmonton Mall is 12,000 m² smaller than the Dubai Mall.
- The Dubai Mall is the most popular. It has 39 million more shoppers per year than Harrods.
- The Dubai Mall is the biggest. It has 870 more shops/departments than Harrods.

	West Edmonton Mall, Canada	Dubai Mall, UAE	Harrods, UK
Opened	1981	¹ __2008__	1849
Size	² _____	502,000m²	20,000 m²
Shoppers per year	32 million	54 million	³ _____
Shops or departments	more than 800	⁴ _____	330

3 What's the problem? Write sentences with *too*, *too much*, *too many* and *(not) enough*.

There aren't enough people. _____

_____

4 Look at the pictures. What is their job? What job are they doing today? Write sentences.

Cameron is a firefighter but today he's working as a vet.

Belinda _____

Sam _____

Jessica _____

5 FINISHED?

1 Read the clues and complete the crossword.

Across

2 There's a nice _picture_ of a mountain on the wall.

5 It's best to put milk and cheese in the _____ .

6 My room is full of _____ with books on them.

7 Grandad is relaxing in his favourite _____ .

Down

1 I put the keys in the chest of _____ .

3 I need to clean the _____ because I dropped food on it!

4 I don't have a dishwasher. I wash the dishes in the _____ .

5 Please don't leave your dirty clothes all over the _____ .

(Crossword grid: 2 Across answer = p i c t u r e)

2 Complete the clues with *as ... as* or *enough* and the adjectives in brackets. Then think of answers for the clues.

1 I'm _as tall as_ (tall) a wardrobe and _wide enough_ (wide) for lots of books. What am I? _a bookcase_

2 I'm _____ (comfortable) a sofa, but I'm not _____ (large) for two people. What am I? _____

3 I'm _____ (soft) a blanket, but I'm _____ (big) to cover the room. What am I? _____

4 I'm exactly _____ (long and wide) the floor, but you probably aren't _____ (tall) to touch me. What am I? _____

3 Find four more phrases in the table. Are they things you have to do or don't have to do? Write four sentences.

drink	lots of	water
eat	TV shows	at school
watch	hard	every night
work	enough	chocolate
sleep	for eight hours	for five hours

I have to drink enough water.

1 _____

2 _____

3 _____

4 _____

4 Look at the pictures. Then find and circle six household chores.

doingtheironingaloadingthedishwasheringdoingthewashing-uppermakingyourbedladcleaningthebathroomnonavacuumingthestairsin

1 Six accidents happened at the campsite yesterday. Complete the words. Then use the letters in circles to find the boy's name.

1 A boy was (s) t u n g by some bees.
2 His father ___ ◯ his head on a tree.
3 His friend ___ ___ ___ ◯ ___ over a ball.
4 His little sister ◯ ___ ___ off her bike.
5 His cousin ___ ___ ◯ ___ ___ his ankle.
6 His big sister ___ ___ ◯ ___ her hair.

The boy's name is ___ ___ ___ ___ .

2 Read the rules and write the places.

1 You must have a ticket before you get on. You shouldn't talk to the driver. If someone old gets on, you should give them your seat. _a bus_

2 You mustn't use your phone and you shouldn't talk to your friends during the show. If you want something to eat or drink, you should buy it before you go in. _____

3 You mustn't take big bottles of liquid. You must take your computer and tablet out of your bag. You shouldn't arrive late, in case it takes a long time. _____

4 You mustn't make a fire. You should look out for dangerous animals and you shouldn't eat any plants that you don't know. You shouldn't leave any rubbish. _____

3 Write the answer to these riddles.

1 If you're very rich, you need this. If you're very poor, you have this. If you eat or drink this, you won't live long. What is it?
nothing

2 If there are three apples and you take away two, how many will you have? _____

3 If Mary's mother's children are called April and May, what is her other child called?
_____

4 If I get wet, you'll get dry. What am I?
_____

5 If you don't break this, you won't be able to use it. What is it? _____

4 Write the parts of the body you can see in these photos.

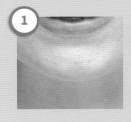  

chin

1 Circle the letters and write the technology words.

1

y	v	b
(e)	(r)	(a)
(s)	(o)	(w)
h	(f)	(t)

software

2

d	o	b
f	w	f
l	n	l
d	a	o

3

t	d	m
a	e	v
s	c	i
j	e	p

4

h	d	a
n	u	o
l	p	l
w	v	q

5

h	m	e
v	j	s
n	a	s
e	g	p

2 Put the letters in order to complete sentences 1–4. Then put the blue letters in order to complete sentence 5.

1

2

3

4

1 Someone has taken her laptop. (ntkae)
2 He hasn't _____ his phone. (cgehard)
3 They've _____ their tablet. (tols)
4 She's _____ the screen on her phone. (sdehmas)
5 No one _____ a good day!

3 In your opinion, will we have these things in the future? Write sentences using *will/won't*, *might* or *may* and *to* + infinitive.

1 *flying cars – take us on holiday*

We might have flying cars to take us on holiday.

2 *3D-printers – make furniture at home*

3 *hoverboards – get around town*

4 *hologram teachers – teach us at home*

5 *translator headsets – understand and speak any language*

4 Circle seven types of transport and four transport verbs in the train.

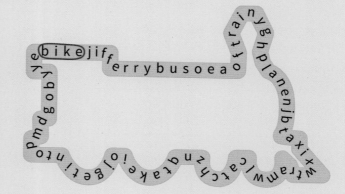

8 FINISHED?

1 Who needs the things in the pictures? Write the jobs in the puzzle. What's the mystery word?

1 | w | r | i | t | e | r |

2

v

3

4

5

6

7

2 Use the code to complete the questions. Then write the answers.

A	B	C	D	E	F	G	H	I	J	K	L	M
✦	♥	☞	◗	⇨	☻	◯	✳	★	☎	♣	✎	✪

N	O	P	Q	R	S	T	U	V	W	X	Y	Z
➡	❖	✖	✚	❄	✈	❀	⊞	⊡	●	✂	✆	➤

1 ⊡★✈★⇨◗ ✳❄⇨ ⊞♣

Have you ever visited the UK ?

2 ●❄★✳✳⇨➡ ✦ ♥❖✦♣

Have you ever _____ ?

_____

3 ✈⇨⇨➡ ✦➡ ⇨✎⇨✖✳✦➡❄

Have you ever _____ ?

_____

4 ✪⇨❄ ✦➡✆❖✳➡⇨ ✳✦❖✪⊞✈

Have you ever _____ ?

_____

3 Circle six reflexive pronouns and eight indefinite pronouns.

l	y	o	u	r	s	e	l	f	s	w	i	e	x	c
t	k	o	s	o	m	e	o	n	e	b	v	i	v	q
o	e	s	e	v	e	r	y	o	n	e	v	s	a	v
m	y	s	e	l	f	a	e	c	r	d	e	j	b	q
t	s	h	u	s	e	y	n	a	v	r	e	v	m	n
h	m	e	n	a	o	t	g	y	e	t	t	q	e	o
e	p	r	a	p	t	w	o	h	t	e	h	r	y	t
m	w	s	n	i	z	k	w	w	a	h	e	g	r	h
s	f	e	y	e	s	o	m	e	t	h	i	n	g	i
e	m	l	w	r	n	a	w	i	w	g	w	n	u	n
l	c	f	h	r	d	e	l	y	t	w	i	e	g	g
v	o	h	e	t	z	e	r	r	p	s	s	v	s	h
e	o	j	r	y	v	e	k	y	g	y	e	u	m	f
s	s	g	e	v	v	d	p	b	b	x	n	l	b	g
e	h	t	h	e	h	i	m	s	e	l	f	h	f	t

4 Put the letters in the inventor's machine in order to complete the phrasal verbs.

1 carry on
2 _____ up to
3 take _____ in
4 come up _____
5 set _____

6 _____ out
7 _____ up
8 _____ up
9 _____ up with
10 _____ off

cayrr ookl
ratp hwit
fof

krow veig
tse peke
hows

1 Look at the photos. Write the missing instruments and the genre of music you think they are playing.

saxophone

folk

2 Follow the lines and write sentences about what the people are and aren't going to do.

Danny / buy

Danny isn't going to buy a keyboard.
He's going to buy a guitar.

Chloe / play

Pablo / take up

Olivia and Leo / learn

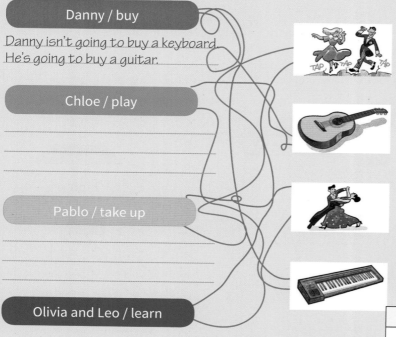

3 Use the code. Write Sophie and Matt's secret plans for the weekend.

1

Sophie

K'o oggvkpi oa htkgpfu qp Ucvwtfc
gxgpkpi cpf yg'tg iqkpi vq ugg c
hkno cv vjg ekpgoc.
I'm meeting my friends on Saturday.

2

Matt

Dgp cpf K ctg iqkpi vq c tqem
eqpegtv kp Nkxgtrqqn. Qwt vtckp
ngcxgu cv vjtgg q'enqem.

C	D	E	F	G	H	I	J	K	L	M	N	O
A	**B**	**C**	**D**	**E**	**F**	**G**	**H**	**I**	**J**	**K**	**L**	**M**
P	Q	R	S	T	U	V	W	X	Y	Z	A	B
N	**O**	**P**	**Q**	**R**	**S**	**T**	**U**	**V**	**W**	**X**	**Y**	**Z**

4 Circle five music genres and five dance styles.

B	A	L	L	E	T	D	A	N	C	I	N	G	E	O	D	O	G	J	W	A	E	M	U
J	T	A	P	D	A	N	C	I	N	G	L	A	C	I	S	S	A	L	C	B	J	N	Y
Z	A	G	U	R	U	G	F	E	C	N	A	D	K	A	E	R	B	V	Y	M	I	L	F
S	G	Z	E	O	W	O	G	Q	F	P	B	X	H	W	S	W	I	N	G	U	U	L	O
Q	G	V	Z	C	L	E	S	E	L	F	M	R	A	R	Z	T	J	Y	K	Z	F	F	A
K	P	B	M	K	G	Q	F	O	R	Y	B	S	X	I	V	B	K	S	O	N	C	O	K

STARTER VOCABULARY BANK

Free time and hobbies

chat online	listen to music	take photos
download songs	make cakes/videos	write a blog
go shopping	play an instrument	
go for a bike ride	read books/	
hang out with friends	magazines	

Sport

athletics	sailing
basketball	swimming
gymnastics	table tennis
hockey	volleyball
rugby	windsurfing

1 **Correct the verbs in these sentences.**

1 Do you want to play _____ swimming with us?

2 My mum often makes _____ shopping on Saturday.

3 We go _____ basketball at school.

4 I usually do _____ photos with my phone.

5 Does your brother play _____ athletics?

Personal possessions

bus pass

camera

headphones

keys

laptop

money

passport

phone

portable charger

tablet

2 **Are the sentences _T_ (true) or _F_ (false)?**

1 You need a passport to make a cake. ____

2 You use a camera to download songs. ____

3 You can use headphones to listen to music. ____

4 You use a portable charger to write a blog. ____

5 You can use your laptop to chat online. ____

6 You can use your phone to read books. ____

🛡️ LEARN TO LEARN

Making vocabulary flashcards
Make vocabulary flashcards to help you learn new words. Draw a picture on one side and write the word on the other.

3 Use the flashcards you made in class. Take turns to pick up a flashcard, look at the picture and name the things. Ask your partner questions about the things they've got.

Bus pass. Have you got a bus pass?   Yes, I have.   Where is it?   It's ...

1 VOCABULARY BANK

TV shows

cartoon

chat show

comedy

cookery show

documentary

drama

game show

on-demand series

reality show

soap opera

sports show

the news

1 Complete the table so it is true for you. Discuss with your partner.

	Name of show	Type of show
I love		
I like		
I don't mind		
I hate		

> I love **MasterChef Junior**. It's a **cookery show**.

> Me too! I watch it every week.

> I like **Futurama**. It's a **cartoon**.

> I hate it. It's boring, but my brother watches it.

Making movies

actor	costume	director	make-up artist	set
camera operator	(digital) camera	lights	script	sound engineer

2 Who or what are these people talking about? Write the correct making movies words.

1 She can make a 30-year-old actor look like an old man. _____

2 The clothes they wear are amazing! _____

3 The conversations between the girl and her mother sound so real. _____

4 He's so good at his job. You can hear every noise the animals make. _____

5 She sometimes tells the actors to speak louder. _____

 LEARN TO LEARN

Look, cover, remember
Use the look, cover, remember technique to help you learn new vocabulary.

3 Look at the words for making movies for one minute. Then close your book. Write the words you can remember in your notebook. Compare with a partner.

The weather

cloudy

cold

dry

foggy

hot

icy

rainy

snowy

stormy

sunny

warm

wet

windy

1 Complete the puzzle and find the mystery word.

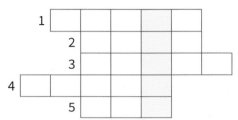

1 We can go skiing when it's _____ .
2 Water that falls from the sky is _____ .
3 We can go to the beach when the weather is _____ .
4 A grey or white thing in the sky is a _____ .
5 A place is _____ when it doesn't rain.
   The mystery word is _____ .

Useful objects

blanket	cup	knife	pillow	spoon
bowl	fork	lamp	plate	toothbrush
comb	hairbrush	mirror	scissors	

2 Circle the correct word.

1 I used a *spoon / knife / fork* to cut the meat.
2 He put his head on the *pillow / lamp / blanket*.
3 Can you put these biscuits on a *bowl / cup / plate*, please?
4 I need to clean my teeth. Where's my *comb / hairbrush / toothbrush*?
5 Anna looked at her hair in the *mirror / lamp / scissors*.

🛡 LEARN TO LEARN

Connecting words with places
When you learn new words, think of places where you can use them. This will help you remember them.

3 Write the useful objects you can usually find in these places.

1 bedroom: _____
2 kitchen: _____
3 bathroom: _____

Adjectives of feeling

afraid

angry

bored

embarrassed

excited

lonely

nervous

surprised

tired

upset

worried

1 Write the correct adjective to describe how these people are feeling.

1 Dad wants to go to bed. He really needs to sleep. _____

2 I don't like this club because we do the same things every week. _____

3 Sasha is crying because she lost her phone. _____

4 All his friends go to a different school. _____

5 Did you really see Katie this morning? I thought she was in New York! _____

Prepositions of movement

across along	between down	into off	out of over	past through	under up

2 Match 1–5 with a–e.

1 Mum was angry when she found dirty clothes under   a her bike.

2 Polly was afraid to walk through   b its box.

3 I was very excited when I took the present out of   c my brother's bed.

4 Chloe was embarrassed when she fell off   d a busy road.

5 Dad was worried because the children had to go across   e the woods.

🛡 LEARN TO LEARN

Practise new words in context

Try to practise new words in sentences you often use. This will help you remember them.

🔊 3 Choose four prepositions and write four sentences that are true for you. Then tell your partner.

1 _____

2 _____

3 _____

4 _____

My bus goes past the swimming pool on the way to school.

Money verbs

borrow	cost	lend	pay	sell
change	earn	owe	save	spend

1 Complete the sentences with the money verbs. Sometimes there is more than one possible answer. Ask and answer with a partner.

1 Who _____ for your phone?

2 Do you usually _____ all your pocket money?

3 Do you do any jobs to _____ money?

4 Do you ever _____ money from your friends?

5 How much does a good laptop _____?

Caring jobs

carer

charity worker

firefighter

lawyer

lifeguard

nurse

paramedic

police officer

refuse collector

surgeon

vet

volunteer

2 Are the sentences *T* (true) or *F* (false)?

1 Carers help old or ill people. _____

2 Paramedics usually look after animals. _____

3 Lifeguards often work at big football matches. _____

4 Nurses often work in hospitals. _____

5 Lawyers are people who work, but don't earn money. _____

🛡 LEARN TO LEARN

Stress patterns
Knowing the stress pattern of a word can help you pronounce it and understand it when people say it.

3 Circle the correct stress pattern for each word.

1 firefighter   ooO   Ooo   oOo

2 paramedic   ooOo   Oooo   oOoo

3 police officer   oO ooo   oo Ooo   oo ooO

4 volunteer   ooO   oOo   Ooo

5 refuse collector   oo Ooo   oO ooo   Oo ooo

5 VOCABULARY BANK

Furniture

armchair

bookcase

carpet

ceiling

chest of drawers

cupboard

desk

floor

fridge

picture

shelves

sink

wardrobe

1 Circle eight items of furniture.

sinkwerpicturemokfloorcdcupboardaltceilingquicarpetbifbookcasepumwardrobeas

Household chores

clean (the kitchen)	do the washing-up	make your bed
do the ironing	empty (the washing machine)	tidy up (the living room)
do the washing	load the dishwasher	vacuum (the carpet)

2 Cover the list of household chores. Circle the correct words.

1 Could you do the *bed / carpet / washing-up*, please?

2 Ben helped me load the *dishwasher / cupboards / bookcase*.

3 I make my *ironing / bed / washing* every morning.

4 We really need to clean the *washing / bed / kitchen*.

5 She usually vacuums the *bed / carpet / cupboard* once a week.

🛡 LEARN TO LEARN

Using spidergrams
Creating spidergrams can help you to remember new words that are related.

3 Complete the spidergram with verbs for household chores. Some chores can go with more than one room.

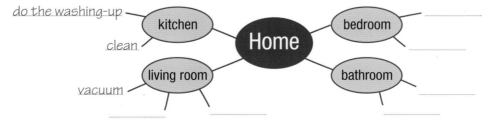

Accidents and injuries

be bitten (by a mosquito)
be stung (by a bee)
break (your leg)

bruise (your leg)
burn (your hand)
cut (your finger)

fall off (your horse)
hit (your head)
scratch (your arm)

slip
sprain (your ankle)
trip over (a chair)

1 Put the words in the correct order to make sentences.

1 his / my / dad / cooker / burned / hand / the / on

_____

2 broke / horse / fell / her / and / her / leg / off / Lena

_____

3 Sara / over / tripped / sprained / and / ankle / her

_____

4 hit / his / cupboard / on / a / Dan / door / head

_____

5 neck / my / I / stung / on / by / a / was / bee

_____

Parts of the body

cheek

chest

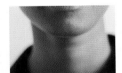
chin

elbow

forehead

heel

knee

neck

shoulder

teeth

toe

wrist

2 Underline the incorrect word.

1 You can break your *cheek / toe / wrist*.
2 You can sprain your *wrist / ankle / forehead*.
3 You can be bitten on your *elbow / teeth / shoulder*.
4 Your *neck / chin / forehead* is part of your face.
5 Your *heel / toe / knee* is part of your foot.
6 Your *shoulder / wrist / neck* is part of your arm.

🛡 LEARN TO LEARN

Making a picture dictionary
Drawing and labelling pictures helps you remember new vocabulary.

3 Close your book. Draw a person in your notebook. Label the parts of the body. Then check to see if you have remembered all the words.

Communication and technology

app	device	emoji	screen	software	video chat
chip	download	message	social media	upload	

1 Match 1–5 with a–e.

1 I sent Julia a message
2 Ibrahim downloaded an app
3 I'm going to upload
4 Bella had a long video chat
5 She added an emoji

a with her cousin.
b the photos from our trip.
c because she left her keys at my house.
d to show she was joking.
e to help him learn English words.

Getting around

catch/get/take (a plane) get into (a taxi) get off (a bus) get on (a train) get out of (a car) go by (tram) go on foot

2 Look at the photos of people getting around. How often do you do these things? Complete the table. Compare with a partner.

Every day	
Often	
Sometimes	
Never	

 **LEARN TO LEARN**

Collocations
Some words are often used together – we call these collocations. Learn them as phrases.

3 <u>Underline</u> and correct a mistake in each sentence. There is sometimes more than one possible answer.

1 You should get out of the bus near the castle.

_____

2 Dad goes to work on train.

_____

3 We got on a taxi and went to the airport.

_____

4 They went by a plane to Japan.

_____

5 Get in the train at Portland station.

_____

Exceptional jobs and qualities

athlete

businessman/
businesswoman

composer

inventor

mathematician

scientist

surgeon

writer

creativity
determination
intelligence
skill
strength
talent

1 Choose two exceptional jobs you think you would be good at and two you think you would be bad at. Write the qualities each job needs. Compare with a partner.

1 _____
2 _____
3 _____
4 _____

Phrasal verbs: achievement

carry on	give up	look up to	set up	take part in
come up with	keep up with	set off	show off	work out

2 Complete the sentences with the phrasal verbs.

1 Jack _____ his older brother, who is an amazing mathematician.
2 My maths homework was very difficult and in the end I had to _____.
3 My sister _____ a great idea for earning money.
4 Sophia walks very quickly. I can't _____ her.
5 My grandmother _____ this business in 1960.

🛡 LEARN TO LEARN

Personalising vocabulary

When you learn new words, use them in sentences to talk about your life. This will help you remember them.

3 Choose three of the phrasal verbs for achievement and write sentences about people you know. Compare with a partner.

1 _____
2 _____
3 _____

My cousin is a businesswoman and she set up a business with her friend.   *I took part in my school play last year.*

Musical instruments and genres

classical	jazz	bass	keyboard	trumpet
folk	reggae	drums	microphone	violin
hip-hop	rock	guitar	saxophone	

1 What am I? Write the musical instrument.

1 I am round and you hit me with sticks. _____

2 I make the singer sound louder. _____

3 I have black and white parts that you press with your fingers. _____

4 I am a very loud instrument. You blow into me and I have three parts you press with your fingers. _____

5 I have four strings. You hold me against your neck. _____

Dance styles

ballet dancing

ballroom dancing

breakdance

country dancing

disco dancing

modern dance

salsa dancing

swing

tap dancing

zumba

2 Are the sentences *T* (true) or *F* (false)?

1 You do ballroom dancing with a partner. ____

2 Breakdance is a slow type of dancing. ____

3 Folk music is often used for disco dancing. ____

4 You need special shoes for ballet dancing. ____

5 Tap dancing makes a noise on the floor. ____

LEARN TO LEARN

Saying collocations out loud

When you learn new vocabulary, say the words out loud. This will help you remember them.

3 What types of dancing do you like? Order the dance styles from favourite (1) to least favourite (10). Compare lists with your partner.

1 _____   6 _____

2 _____   7 _____

3 _____   8 _____

4 _____   9 _____

5 _____   10 _____

The legend of
El Dorado

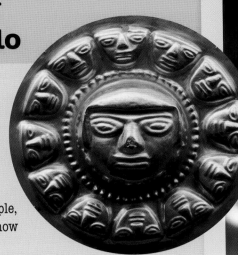

1 Look at the title and picture and discuss the questions.

1 Have you heard of El Dorado?

2 What and where do you think it is?

2 Read the text. Check your answers to Exercise 1.

2.12

3 Complete the sentences with years.

1 ___1520s___ – Spanish conquistadors first heard about the Muisca people.

2 _____ – They first went to look for El Dorado.

3 _____ – They searched Lake Guatavita for gold.

4 _____ – Sir Walter Raleigh failed to find El Dorado.

5 _____ – Alexander von Humboldt proved the site at Lake Parime did not exist.

4 Why did the Europeans want to explore and control the Americas? Discuss with a partner.

5 Match the words in **bold** with the definitions.

1 a long search for something that may not exist or is difficult to find _____

2 a small flat boat, often made of wood _____

3 an old story _____

4 a fight during a war, usually to take control of a place _____

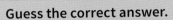

Explore it!

Guess the correct answer.

People once believed there was gold worth … in Lake Guatavita.

a $1 million   b $50 million   c $300 million

Find another interesting fact about a legend. Then write a question for your partner to answer.

In the 1500s, Europeans were discovering and trying to take control of the Americas. In the 1520s, Spanish conquistadors heard about the Muisca people, who lived in what is now Colombia.

The stories suggested that the Muisca had a huge amount of gold. When they chose a new chief, they covered him in gold and sailed him on a **raft** into the middle of Lake Guatavita. The chief put all the gold into the lake as a gift for the gods.

In 1537, the Spanish decided to look for the chief, who they named 'El Dorado', but without success. Then in 1545, they looked for gold in Lake Guatavita. They discovered a few objects, and they became sure that there was a whole city of gold somewhere in the Amazon jungle. People started to refer to the golden city as El Dorado.

Many people looked for El Dorado over the centuries. These included the British explorer Sir Walter Raleigh. In 1617, on his second expedition to South America, he fought a **battle** with the Spanish on the Orinoco River, as both the British and the Spanish searched for El Dorado. The British king was unhappy about this conflict and executed Raleigh on his return.

The **myth** of El Dorado continued to grow. Maps in the seventeenth and eighteenth centuries even showed the city next to a legendary lake, Lake Parime. But nobody ever found it, and in 1803 the German explorer Alexander von Humboldt disproved the existence of this site.

After hundreds of failed expeditions, people finally realised that El Dorado never existed. The phrase 'looking for El Dorado' means to go on a hopeless **quest**.

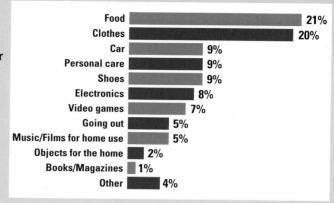

The best things in life are (nearly) free

There is no doubt that money is **essential** to daily life. People earn money to buy food, pay the **bills** or save for something special like a holiday or present. Life becomes extremely difficult for people when there isn't enough money for their basic needs.

However, many people spend too much money on items they do not need. Marketing and advertising **encourage** people to buy an enormous range of products and services, and these days, with 24-hour internet access, it is easier than ever to spend money at the touch of a button.

How American teenagers spend their money according to a recent survey

Category	%
Food	21%
Clothes	20%
Car	9%
Personal care	9%
Shoes	9%
Electronics	8%
Video games	7%
Going out	5%
Music/Films for home use	5%
Objects for the home	2%
Books/Magazines	1%
Other	4%

Some people believe that consuming so much is unhealthy and we should make an effort to find interests do not cost anything at all. If you want to do this, there are a number of options, and a good way to start is by looking at local websites. There are many free events for local communities and you just need to select an activity that interests you. You could choose from music, dance, sport, art, tourism, walking and many, many more.

Of course, you need access to a computer or phone to check a website. This costs money, but if it helps you to save money in the longer term, then it is a good **investment**. Why not have a look today? It may be the first step in reducing your spending and starting a new low-cost life.

1 Discuss the questions.

1 Why do we need money?
2 What kinds of things can we do in our free time without money?

🎧 2 Read the article. Are your ideas in Exercise 1 mentioned?
4.12

3 Are the sentences *T* (true) or *F* (false)?

1 People need money for their basic needs. __T__
2 Teenagers don't need holidays or presents. ____
3 US teenagers spend less than a quarter of their money on clothes. ____
4 We can use technology to find free events. ____
5 If you want to save money, you sometimes have to spend a bit first. ____

4 Complete the sentences with the words in bold.

1 I bought a cheap phone to save money, but it was a bad _____ because it broke and I had to buy a new one.
2 That video game isn't an _____ item. I think you should save your money.
3 Please don't _____ Ben to buy any more trainers. He's already got plenty of pairs.
4 Lisa has almost no money left each month after she pays the _____.

Explore it!

Guess the correct answer.

In the UK, girls aged 13 to 15 spend on average £1.70 per week on personal care. Boys spend …

a £1.60.   b 10 pence.   c £4.00.

Find another interesting fact about teen spending. Then write a question for your partner to answer.

SMALL BUT DEADLY

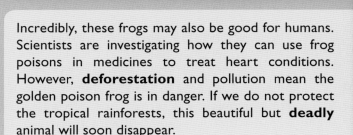

Imagine you are trekking through a rainforest. You're amazed at the rich variety of wildlife, although you're nervous about meeting a jaguar or a boa constrictor. Suddenly, you see something bright and yellow on a plant. You move closer and realise that it's a tiny frog. 'Frogs aren't dangerous,' you think, and you hold out your hand …

Stop! The animal in front of you is *Phyllobates terribilis*, or the golden poison frog. It is the most poisonous land animal in the world.

The golden poison frog is an amphibian that lives in the rainforests of Colombia. It is only about 5 cm long and weighs less than 25 grams. It is a **carnivore**, and it eats ants, beetles and centipedes that only live in the rainforest. Scientists believe this specific diet produces the poison that the frogs secrete from their backs. If a human touches a golden poison frog, it can cause **swelling**, nausea, paralysis or even death.

Incredibly, these frogs may also be good for humans. Scientists are investigating how they can use frog poisons in medicines to treat heart conditions. However, **deforestation** and pollution mean the golden poison frog is in danger. If we do not protect the tropical rainforests, this beautiful but **deadly** animal will soon disappear.

So, if you see one of these creatures in the jungle, keep your distance and leave it alone. Then you will both stay safe.

1 Look at the title and photo. What information can you guess about this frog?

🎧 6.13 2 Read the article. Were your ideas correct?

3 Complete the fact file about the golden poison frog.

SCIENTIFIC NAME:	1	*Phyllobates terribilis*
TYPE OF ANIMAL:	2	
SIZE:	3	
WEIGHT:	4	
DIET:	5	
HOME:	6	

4 Complete the sentences.
   1 The golden poison frog can hurt people if _____
   _____
   2 It can help people because _____
   _____

5 Complete the sentences with the words in **bold**.
   1 This snake has a _____ bite. It can kill you.
   2 There was _____ on his toe where he was stung. His toe was bigger than usual.
   3 Because of _____, a lot of animals have lost their homes.
   4 An animal that eats meat, like a cat, is a _____.

Explore it! 🖱

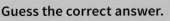

Guess the correct answer.
The golden poison frog has enough poison to kill …
a a cat.   b 20,000 mice.   c an elephant.
Find another interesting fact about a dangerous animal. Then write a question for your partner to answer.

1 Look at the photos. Do you know what the invention is and who invented it?

2 Read the article. Check your answers to Exercise 1.
8.13

3 Put the events in order.

a [1] Farnsworth entered invention competitions.

b [ ] He went to university.

c [ ] He had an idea while he was working on his family's farm.

d [ ] Businesses took up his ideas.

e [ ] He presented a prototype.

f [ ] He worked out a process for making a fully electronic television.

4 Imagine you're going to spend 24 hours without looking at any type of screen. How can you spend your time? Discuss your ideas with a partner.

5 Match the words in **bold** with the definitions.

1 plants that farmers grow _____

2 change slowly over a period of time _____

3 stop doing something before you have completely finished _____

4 first example of an invention _____

Explore it! 🖱

Guess the correct statement.

a After his invention, Philo Farnsworth had a television in every room of his house.

b Philo Farnsworth became one of the first television news presenters.

c Philo Farnsworth didn't like television and didn't allow his family to watch it.

Find another interesting fact about television. Then write a question for your partner to answer.

Philo Farnsworth:
a big influence on the small screen

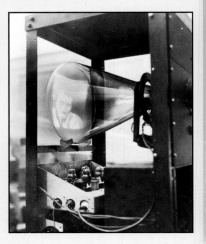

The television is probably the world's most popular form of entertainment. On average, people around the world watch three hours of television per day, and in Europe and North America, this is closer to four hours. But who is responsible for this amazing invention?

It isn't an easy question to answer, because over the years, different people developed different types of televisions. One of these was Philo Farnsworth, a farmer's son from Utah in the USA, who built the first all-electronic TV set. This young man's creativity and determination made a big difference in the development of the small screen.

Farnsworth was always interested in inventions. As a young teenager, he took part in invention competitions and made mechanical gadgets that helped with household chores. In 1921, at the age of 15, he came up with the basic idea for a totally electronic television. He was looking at the parallel lines of **crops** on his family's farm when he realised that he could separate images into parallel lines of light, which he could transform into images.

Farnsworth was a brilliant student, and entered university, but he was forced to **drop out** and work after his father died. However, he continued to work on his invention. Finally, in 1928, he finalised his **prototype** TV. His invention continued to **evolve** and improve, and throughout his career, different companies produced different versions of it. The television continues to evolve quickly – today's flat-screen smart TVs will surely look old-fashioned to future generations.

PRONUNCIATION

UNIT 1
Contractions: *be*

🎧 **1** **Listen and repeat.**
1.04
1. **I am** sitting in my bedroom. > **I'm** sitting in my bedroom.
2. **He is** taking a selfie. > **He's** taking a selfie.
3. **You are** walking on the moon. > **You're** walking on the moon.
4. **We are** listening to music. > **We're** listening to music.

🎧 **2** **Listen and circle the option you hear. Practise**
1.05 **saying the sentences.**
1. *They are / They're* listening to music.
2. *She is / She's* reading a blog.
3. *He is / He's* skiing in France.
4. *You are / You're* watching TV.
5. *It is / It's* eating.

UNIT 2
/t/, /d/ and /ɪd/

🎧 **1** **Listen and repeat.**
2.03
1. /t/ walk**ed** 2. /d/ liv**ed** 3. /ɪd/ want**ed**

2 **Write the verbs in the correct column.**

> ~~agreed~~ arrived changed cooked
> decided helped looked
> survived travelled wanted

1 /t/ or /d/	2 /ɪd/
agreed,	

🎧 **3** **Listen and check.**
2.04

UNIT 3
Word stress in adjectives

1 **How many syllables have these adjectives got?**

afraid [2]   angry [ ]   bored [ ]
nervous [ ]   excited [ ] lonely [ ]
upset [ ]   surprised [ ] tired [ ]

🎧 **2** **Listen and check.**
3.02

3 **Match the words in Exercise 1 with their stress patterns. Complete the table.**

1 oO	2 Oo	3 oOo	4 O
afraid			

🎧 **4** **Listen and repeat the sentences.**
3.03
1. Sam's afraid of dogs.
2. My best friend is very upset.
3. I'm worried about exams.
4. I studied all night and I'm very tired.
5. I feel embarrassed when I forget someone's name.

UNIT 4
Schwa at the end of words

🎧 **1** **Listen and repeat.**
4.06
/ə/ refuse collect**or**   charity work**er**
fitt**er**   bett**er**

🎧 **2** **Listen and repeat the sentences.**
4.07
1. My sister's a firefighter.
2. The teacher is happier than the actor.
3. Life is better when you're healthier.

UNIT 5
have: /f/ vs /v/

🎧 **1** **Listen and circle the option you hear: /f/ or /v/.**
5.08
1. Jenny and Peter **have** to make their beds every day. /f/ / /v/
2. I**'ve** got a new bed. /f/ / /v/
3. George and Helen **have** to make dinner every Saturday. /f/ / /v/
4. Tom doesn't **have** to help in the house. /f/ / /v/
5. **Have** you got a big garden? /f/ / /v/
6. Sam and Dan don't **have** to do much. /f/ / /v/

PRONUNCIATION

2 Listen and repeat the sentences. (5.09)

1 I **have** to do the gardening this weekend.
2 My brothers **have** got a really big wardrobe.
3 We don't **have** to go to school on Monday.
4 We **have** got a bookcase in the living room.
5 Does Liam **have** to do the washing-up?

UNIT 6
/ʌ/ and /ʊ/

1 Listen and repeat. (6.04)

1 /ʌ/ m**u**st m**u**stn't
2 /ʊ/ sh**ou**ld c**oo**k f**u**ll

2 Write the words in the correct column.

~~brother~~ could cousin cut foot put stung

1 /ʌ/	2 /ʊ/
brother,	

3 Listen, check and repeat. (6.05)

4 Listen and repeat the sentences. (6.06)

1 She cut her foot, so she couldn't call her cousin.
2 I must put some books in the cupboard.

UNIT 7
The letter *i*

1 Listen and repeat. (7.03)

1 /ɪ/ ch**i**p f**i**lm k**i**ck
2 /aɪ/ l**i**ke onl**i**ne h**i**

2 Write the words in the correct column.

bike device ~~Internet~~ online printer video wi-fi will write

1 /ɪ/	2 /aɪ/
Internet,	

3 Listen, check and repeat. (7.04)

4 Listen and repeat the sentences. (7.05)

1 James can't get wi-fi, so he hasn't got the Internet.
2 I can watch video online on my new device.

UNIT 8
Intonation in questions

1 Listen and repeat. (8.04)

1 Was Mozart a scientist?
2 Where do you live?
3 Have you cycled 100 km?
4 What did you do last night?

2 Read the interview. Circle where Nick's voice goes up in questions. <u>Underline</u> where it goes down in questions.

NICK   <u>How long have you been a teacher?</u>
MR T   Well, Nick. It's been 20 years now.
NICK   (Really?) That's a long time! Do you like it?
MR T   Yes, but some days are harder than others.
NICK   What do you like best about it?
MR T   The best thing is seeing students improve.
NICK   That's great. Do you think you'll be a teacher for the next 20 years?
MR T   Well, I hope so!

3 Listen, check and repeat. (8.05)

UNIT 9
Sentence stress

1 How many syllables have these sentences got? Then <u>underline</u> the words you think are stressed.

1 We're <u>going</u> to <u>play</u> <u>jazz</u>. ⑥
2 We'll buy a new guitar. ☐
3 Is Jake playing the drums? ☐
4 We're going to a rap concert. ☐

2 Listen, check and repeat. (9.07)

3 Clap the rhythm of these sentences.

1 Do you like reggae?
2 She likes classical music.
3 The concert starts at 8 o'clock.
4 Adam is organising the music.

IRREGULAR VERBS

Infinitive	Past simple	Past participle
be	was / were	been
beat	beat	beaten
become	became	become
begin	began	begun
break	broke	broken
bring	brought	brought
build	built	built
burn	burnt / burned	burnt / burned
buy	bought	bought
catch	caught	caught
choose	chose	chosen
come	came	come
cost	cost	cost
cut	cut	cut
do	did	done
draw	drew	drawn
drink	drank	drunk
drive	drove	driven
eat	ate	eaten
fall	fell	fallen
feed	fed	fed
feel	felt	felt
fight	fought	fought
find	found	found
fly	flew	flown
forget	forgot	forgotten
get	got	got
give	gave	given
go	went	gone
grow	grew	grown
hang	hung	hung
have	had	had
hear	heard	heard
hide	hid	hidden
hit	hit	hit
hold	held	held
keep	kept	kept

Infinitive	Past simple	Past participle
know	knew	known
leave	left	left
lend	lent	lent
lose	lost	lost
make	made	made
meet	met	met
pay	paid	paid
put	put	put
read	read	read
ride	rode	ridden
ring	rang	rung
run	ran	run
say	said	said
see	saw	seen
sell	sold	sold
send	sent	sent
set	set	set
show	showed	shown
shut	shut	shut
sing	sang	sung
sit	sat	sat
sleep	slept	slept
speak	spoke	spoken
spend	spent	spent
stand	stood	stood
swim	swam	swum
take	took	taken
teach	taught	taught
tell	told	told
think	thought	thought
throw	threw	thrown
understand	understood	understood
wake	woke	woken
wear	wore	worn
win	won	won
write	wrote	written

Acknowledgements

The authors and publishers acknowledge the following sources of copyright material and are grateful for the permissions granted. While every effort has been made, it has not always been possible to identify the sources of all the material used, or to trace all copyright holders. If any omissions are brought to our notice, we will be happy to include the appropriate acknowledgements on reprinting and in the next update to the digital edition, as applicable.

Key: CLIL: Content and Language Integrated Learning, ST: Starter; TR: Team Review; U: Unit.

Text

U03: Text about Beth Reekles. Copyright © Beth Reekles. Reproduced with kind permission; U04: Text about Mark Boyle. Copyright © Mark Boyle. Reproduced with kind permission of Jessica Woollard.

Photography

All photographs are sourced from Getty Images.

CLIL: Adam Woolfitt/robertharding/robertharding; claffra/iStock/Getty Images Plus; Jamie Grill; Jacobs Stock Photography Ltd/DigitalVision; studo58/iStock/Getty Images Plus; niphon/iStock/Getty Images Plus; Bjorn Holland/Photodisc; Doug88888/Moment Open; Anakrubah/iStock/Getty Images Plus; Alfredo Maiquez/Lonely Planet Images/Getty Images Plus; robbin0919/iStock/Getty Images Plus; FF: BananaStock/BananaStock;Ken Reid/iStock/Getty Images Plus; mediaphotos/iStock/Getty Images Plus; fotostorm/iStock/Getty Images Plus; PhotoAlto/Milena Boniek/PhotoAlto Agency RF Collections; uniquely india; Manita Charoenpru/EyeEm; Dorling Kindersley/Dorling Kindersley; alle12/E+; Selektor/iStock/Getty Images Plus; nortongo/iStock/Getty Images Plus; Glow Images; Photitos2016/iStock/Getty Images Plus; Ryan McVay/Photodisc; Arthur Baensch/Corbis/Getty Images Plus; moodboard/iStock/Getty Images Plus; Jon Feingersh Photography Inc/DigitalVision; urbancow/iStock/Getty Images Plus; shironosov/iStock/Getty Images Plus; ddukang/iStock/Getty Images Plus; grandriver/E+; ST: Photo and Co/DigitalVision; Image Source/DigitalVisionl; Image Source/Image Source; Fgorgun/iStock/Getty Images Plus; MachineHeadz/iStock/Getty Images Plus; Kritchanut/iStock/Getty Images Plus; Ian Dikhtiar/EyeEm; Thn K Vt Phu Ceriy/EyeEm; SensorSpot/E+; pbombaert/Moment; ABBPhoto/iStock/Getty Images Plus; momokey/iStock/Getty Images Plus; Frederick Bass; Creative Crop/DigitalVision; Richard Newstead/Moment; Terri Lee-Shield Photography/iStock/Getty Images Plus; Nathan Stirk/Getty Images Sport; U1: sutiporn somnam/Moment; inhauscreative/E+; vm/E+; Konstantin Trubavin/Aurora Photos; WLDavies/E+; ARTPUPPY/DigitalVision Vectors; Daviles/iStock/Getty Images Plus; Erik Dreyer/Stone/Getty Images Plus; Newton Daly/DigitalVision; Newton Daly/DigitalVision; Jasmin Merdan/Moment; ullstein bild Dtl; dmbaker/iStock/Getty Images Plus; Westend61; LajosRepasi/iStock/Getty Images Plus; ildarss/iStock/Getty Images Plus; Kcris Ramos/Moment Unreleased; George Konig/Hulton Archive; Mims/RooM; Juanmonino/iStock/Getty Images Plus; J Carter Rinaldi/FilmMagic; Anouk de Maar/iStock/Getty Images Plus; mediaphotos/iStock/Getty Images Plus; Jasper Cole; liangpv/DigitalVision Vectors; simon2579/DigitalVision Vectors; Wibowo Rusli/iStock/Getty Images Plus; davidf/E+; George Morgan/EyeEm U2: Frantois Marclay/Moment; Mitchell Funk/iStock/Getty Images Plus; Laurence Dutton/Stone/Getty Images Plus; Tim Graham/Getty Images News; Pacific Press/LightRocket; AnnaFrajtova/iStock/Getty Images Plus; Archive Holdings Inc/Archive Photos; bradwieland/iStock/Getty Images Plus; DEA PICTURE LIBRARY/De Agostini; Ismailciydem/iStock/Getty Images Plus; Daisy-Daisy/iStock/Getty Images Plus; jiduha/iStock/Getty Images Plus; Bettmann; Print Collector/Hulton Archive; Charly_Morlock/iStock/Getty Images Plus; Fotosearch/Archive Photos; Oleh_Slobodeniuk/E+; Hulton Deutsch/Corbis Historical; mocoo/iStock/Getty Images Plus; U3: Neustockimages/E+; Betsie Van Der Meer/DigitalVision; Steve Debenport/E+; Shinyfamily/iStock/Getty Images Plus; gawrav/E+; Rob Lewine; Zelma Brezinska/EyeEm; ozgurdonmaz/iStock/Getty Images Plus; songdech17/iStock/Getty Images Plus; HEX; Jose Luis Pelaez Inc/DigitalVision; Mark Kerton/Action Plus; Elva Etienne/Moment; DNY59/E+; Sergiy1975/iStock/Getty Images Plus; Maica/iStock/Getty Images Plus; Image_Source/iStock/Getty Images Plus; tomertu/iStock/Getty Images Plus; andresr/iStock/Getty Images Plus; John Gress/Corbis Historical; GK Hart/Vikki Hart/Stone/Getty Images Plus; prudkov/iStock/Getty Images Plus; KidStock/Blend Images; U4: filipefrazao/iStock/Getty Images Plus; jessicaphoto/iStock Unreleased; mtreasure/iStock/Getty Images Plus; Laetizia Haessig/EyeEm; Glow Images, Inc; GCShutter/E+; KAZUHIRO NOGI/AFP; Chuvashov Maxim/Image Source; RUSS ROHDE/iStock/Getty Images Plus; Oliver Helbig/EyeEm; Matt Cardy/Getty Images News; Sally Anscombe/Moment; John Wood Photography/iStock/Getty Images Plus; RichLegg/E+; Bill Stormont/iStock/Getty Images Plus; Asanka Brendon Ratnayake/iStock/Getty Images Plus; asiseeit/E+; Wavebreakmedia/iStock/Getty Images Plus;Jeff Dunn/iStock/Getty Images Plus; FS Productions; Razvan/iStock/Getty Images Plus; fotostorm/iStock/Getty Images Plus; Gregory Shamus/Getty Images Sport; dolgachov/iStock/Getty Images Plus; Sladic/iStock/Getty Images Plus; ColorBlind Images/The Image Bank/Getty Images Plus; U5: Martine Roch/Moment; Cristiano Gala/iStock/Getty Images Plus; PhotoAlto/Jerome Gorin/PhotoAlto Agency RF Collections; Jbryson/iStock/Getty Images Plus; Juanmonino/iStock/Getty Images Plus; KatarzynaBialasiewicz/iStock/Getty Images Plus; Alvis Upitis/Photographer's Choice RF; Klaus Mellenthin/Westend61; Paul Almasy/Corbis Historical; ihorga/iStock/Getty Images Plus; ra-photos/E+; Johner Images/Brand X Pictures; Richard Newstead/Moment; Cavan Images; andresr/E+; Himsyah Inchakep/EyeEm; David Santiago Garcia/Aurora; mocoo/iStock/Getty Images Plus; U6: Barcroft Media; Viktoria Rodriguez/EyeEm; shannonstent/E+; maerzkind/iStock/Getty Images Plus; James Gritz/Photodisc; vandervelden/iStock/Getty Images Plus; Hill Street Studios/DigitalVision; Westend61;Robert Niedring/MITO images; Anton Petrus/Moment; Pavliha/E+; SteveMcsweeny/iStock/Getty Images Plus; Frans Lemmens/Corbis Unreleased; JuhaHuiskonen/E+; David Fettes/iStock/Getty Images Plus; ONOKY - Brooke Auchincloss/Brand X Pictures; Jef Wodniack/iStock/Getty Images Plus; moodboard/Getty Images Plus; Fotofeeling/Westend61; Phil Boorman/Cultura; T. Eidenweil/imageBROKER; Gordon Scammell/LOOP IMAGES/Corbis Documentary; Alistair Berg/Stone; U7: PhotoAlto/Frederic Cirou/PhotoAlto Agency RF Collections; DanHallman/iStock/Getty Images Plus; Maskot; AntonioFrancois/iStock/Getty Images Plus; Liam Norris/iStock/Getty Images Plus; VLIET/iStock Unreleased; Johner Images; Mike Harrington/DigitalVision; uniquely india; Javier Pierini/Stockbyte; Design Pics/Ron Nickel; SolStock/E+; dmbaker/iStock/Getty Images Plus; Bedrin-Alexander/iStock/Getty Images Plus; PhotoAlto Agency RF Collections/Michele Constantini; fstop123/iStock/Getty Images Plus; LeoPatrizi/E+; Wavebreakmedia Ltd/Lightwavemedia; SeanPavonePhoto/iStock/Getty Images Plus; Junior Gonzalez; monsitj/iStock/Getty Images Plus; metamorworks/iStock/Getty Images Plus; Steve Vidler/SuperStock; Mongkol Chuewong/Moment; monkeybusinessimages/iStock/Getty Images Plus; Donald Iain Smith; PhotoAlto/Michele Constantini/PhotoAlto Agency RF Collections; U8: Mieke Dalle/iStock/Getty Images Plus; Portra/DigitalVision; Hero Images; LightFieldStudios/iStock/Getty Images Plus; Jovo Marjanovic/EyeEm; Ariel Skelley/DigitalVision; technotr/iStock/Getty Images Plus; Hero Images/Hero Images; Diverse Images/Universal Images Group; ArielSkelley/DigitalVision; Flashpop/DigitalVision; Westend61/Brand X Pictures; gbh007/iStock/Getty Images Plus; Kristine JoyTropicales/Moment Open; South China Morning Post; digitalskillet/iStock/Getty Images Plus; Bloom Productions/iStock/Getty Images Plus; Gary Bennett/EyeEm; Denis Goujon/EyeEm; abadonian/iStock/Getty Images Plus; mocoo/iStock/Getty Images Plus; U9: Bennett Raglin/BET/Getty Images Entertainment; Photodisc; SensorSpot/E+; Lane Oatey/Blue Jean Images; Claudiad/E+; Tim Graham/The Image Bank/Getty Images Plus; jonya/E+; Stephanie Nantel/Moment; Peathegee Inc; Bim/E+; FatCamera/iStock/Getty Images Plus; Patrick Riviere/Getty Images Entertainment; Hill Street Studios/DigitalVision; Tony Anderson/The Image Bank/Getty Images Plus; Paul Marotta/Getty Images Entertainment; Valeriy_G/iStock/Getty Images Plus; Prisma Bildagentur/Universal Images Group;Education Images/Universal Images Group;Neil Farrin/AWL Images; Lebedinski/iStock/Getty Images Plus; carlosbezz/iStock/Getty Images Plus; J-Elgaard/iStock/Getty Images Plus; sihuo0860371/iStock/Getty Images Plus; Jonathan Kitchen/Photographer's Choice RF; RapidEye/E+; 8213erika/iStock/Getty Images Plus; Christian Jakubaszek/Getty Images Entertainment; Troy Aossey/Taxi; drbimages/iStock/Getty Images Plus; George Shelley/Corbis; Electra-K-Vasileiadou/E+; Nigel Roddis/Getty Images News; Hill Street Studios/Blend Images; VBS: nidwlw/iStock/Getty Images Plus; Ilya_Starikov/iStock/Getty Images Plus; ozanuysal/iStock/Getty Images Plus; Emrah Turudu/Photographer's Choice RF; Karunyapas Krueklad/EyeEm; Peter Dazeley/Photographer's Choice/Getty Images Plus; Gen Sadakane/EyeEm; scanrail/iStock/Getty Images Plus; sirastock/iStock/Getty Images Plus;daboost/iStock/Getty Images Plus; VB1: yogysic/DigitalVision Vectors; simonkr/E+; Kondo Photography/Cultura; Thomas Barwick/DigitalVision; amygdala_imagery/iStock Unreleased;Elena Peremet/Moment; Michael Cogliantry/The Image Bank/Getty Images Plus;scyther5/iStock/Getty Images Plus; GoodLifeStudio/E+; Caspar Benson; Caiaimage/Chris Ryan; Tashi-Delek/E+; VB2: TobiasAckeborn/Moment;Westend61; cinoby/E+;Bobby Sanderson/EyeEm; Ian Spanier/Image Source; JianGang Wang/iStock Unreleased; Matt Mawson/Moment; Alex Potemkin/E+; Australian Land, City, People Scape Photographer/Moment; Maskot; Johner Images - Fridh, Conny/Brand X Pictures Douglas Sacha/Moment Open Maya Karkalicheva/Moment; VB3: eelnosiva/iStock/Getty Images Plus; Westend61; J-Elgaard/E+; laflor/E+; andresr/E+; Image Source; AaronAmat/iStock/Getty Images Plus; Wavebreakmedia/iStock/Getty Images Plus; GoodLifeStudio/iStock/Getty Images Plus; Shoji Fujita/DigitalVision; Slonov/E+; VB4: SilviaJansen/E+; Steve Debenport/E+;Frances Andrijich/Photolibrary/Getty Images Plus; Highwaystarz-Photography/iStock/Getty Images Plus; Ken Seet/Corbis/VCG; Shapecharge/iStock/Getty Images Plus; Tashi-Delek/E+; kali9/E+; PeopleImages/E+; Sean Justice/Stockbyte; Skynesher/E+;